GETTING DOWN
TO EARTH

BY

HELENE SMITH

*In commemoration of the Tenth Anniversary
of the Hanna's Town archeological and
historical project, 1970-1980*

ILLUSTRATIONS

BY

GREGORY MARTIN SMITH

WESTMORELAND COUNTY HISTORICAL SOCIETY
1980

COPYRIGHT © 1980 BY HELENE SMITH

LIBRARY OF CONGRESS
CATALOG CARD No.: 80-53757

Smith, Helene
Getting down to earth.

Greensburg, Pa.: Westmoreland County
Historical Society

132 p.
8011   800925

ISBN 0-9604966-0-2

PREFACE

Barely a dozen years ago the name of Hanna's Town was almost unknown except for a few specialists in local history, and people living near where the town once stood. Today, largely through the archeological work at the site and historical research which this has encouraged, Hanna's Town is recognized as a place of small size but of great importance—the first center of English justice west of the Allegheny Mountains and a principal rallying place for those brave men and women who risked their very lives to help create a new nation, and to maintain for it a foothold in the west, so necessary to later expansion. It has been a privilege for me to have some small part in this achievement.

A book of this kind is seldom entirely the work of the author, and this one is no exception. I happily take this opportunity to express my gratitude and heartfelt thanks to those who have made this work possible.

First, to the Westmoreland County Historical Society, which initiated the Hanna's Town excavation that first interested me in this field (particularly to its President, Edward Nowlin); to the Katherine Mabis McKenna Foundation, which supported this publication; to Alex G. McKenna; Richard J. Flickinger; and Robert Kendra. For advice and time given to the reading of the manuscript, I would like to thank George Chappars, Jake Grimm, Edward Nowlin, Sandra Nowlin, R.E. Porteous, Wayne Smith, and George Swetnam.

Many people have been involved in and contributed time and effort to the Hanna's Town archeological and historical project. An easy out for the author would be to say they have been far too numerous to list, and instead refer to the group in a general way. I have not chosen the easy way out. The list added as an appendix includes, so far as I can discover or recall, all the volunteers and friends of the Hanna's Town dig from its beginning to the present. I apologize to anyone I may have missed. For those who cannot find their names in the list—perhaps they can find themselves in the narrative, instead—either by name or similitude.

HELENE SMITH

ACKNOWLEDGMENTS

This list contains the names of all those who have given assistance to the Hanna's Town dig during its first ten years. It has been compiled not only from the author's memory, but after making inquiries of many of those most closely associated with this project. If any names have been omitted it is because numerous memories have failed.

Adams, Hazel
Adams, Peggy
Albright, Marge and Barb
Albright, Wilbur, and John
Allen, Gloria
Anderson, Sheri
Andrachick, Valerie

Bail, Ethel
Baily, Evelyn
Baker, Tom-
Barnett, Henry
Barnett, Laura
Bartlow, Judy and Arthur
Bell, Terry
Bennett, David
Berry, Betty
Bittner, Richard
Blansett, Liz
Blauvelt, Bill
Blauvelt, Doris
Blystone, John W.
Boy Scout Troop, 403
  Greensburg
Brabosky, Dave
Bradbury, Andrew
Brady, George D.
Brentzel, Wayne
Brown, Lorraine M.
Brueggemann, Tami
Brunot, Debbie
Bugica, Gregory J.
Buganski, Monica, R.
Bumbera, Larry
Burger, Gene
Burger, "Jack" (John)

Caccia, Susan
Caesar, Robert, Doug, and Jeff
Camp Sequanota
Campbell, Dorothy
Campbell, Marlene

Carris, Mary Jane
Chabal, Dave
Cherry, David
Cholock, Annette Yasem
Cholock, Dennis
Cholock, Peter
Cibik, David
Ciccotelli, Patrick A.
Costello, Chuck
Crystaloski, Brian
Cunningham, Aline
Cunningham, B.
Cunningham, Charles
Cunningham, Charles Jr.
Cunningham, Eleanor
Cunningham, Joe
Curry, Diane

Dargi, Jeff
DeMaria, Mike
Dibas, Joan
Dibas, Matt
DiCrisio, Charlene
Doak, Frank
Doak, Pam
Dohey, Jerry G. Jr.
Dudzik, Dennis
Dunlap, Andrew B.

Ebert, Tom
Elda, Mary Ann
Elizabeth Hanna Guild
Eskut, Marie Anna

Fagan, Lisa
Falcon, James
Ferretti, Joy R.
Fields, Charles
Fields, Linda
Fields, Peggy
Fink, Red
Forbes Road Fire Department
Forish, Linda

Forsyth, B.
Foster, Mark
Fritz, Lee Ann
Garofola, Cindy
Ginter, Joseph F.
Glasser, Wendy
Greenawalt, Jerry
Griffith, Becky
Griffith, Kathy
Grimm, Jake
Guthrie, Tracy
Haeflein, Mari
Hahn, Brenda
Hahn, Ed
Haile, David
Haile, Harriet
Haile, Katherine
Haile, Walter
Hanna, Charles
Hanna, Ed
Hannastown Fire Department
Harrold, Linda
Hastings, Iris
Hawks, Cathy and Jonathan
Headen, David
Heintzelman, Cy
Hellferich, Dale
Helman, Dan
Hill, Bob
Hill, Karin
Hill, Margot
Himler, Lenny
Hindman, David P.
Hughes, Bill
Hughes, Ruth
Isaac, Peter
Iscrupe, William
Jamison, Mandy
Johnson, David S.
Kallaugher, John
Kamenic, Lynn M.
Kaufman, Gretchen M.
Kaufman, Jean
Keill, Angela
Kendra, Arlene
Kendra, Robert
Kent Family
Kindelberger, Sheryl
Kirshner, Sue and Thomas

Kite, Judy
Koch, Carl
Kraft, Jude
Kubas, Frank
Kubit, Brian
Kubit, Chuck J.
Kubit, Eric
Kubit, Lucy
Kuinszyinsky, Elizabeth

Lace, Art
Lace, Pat
Lavely, Beth
Lectley, Dave
Leyh, Don R. and Jody
Leyh, Thomas S.
Lichter, John
Light, Connie
Light, Dale
Linko, David
Lowstetter, Debbie

Magill, Linda
Maline, Charles
Malkames, Jean
Malkames, Judy
Maloney, Sherel
Manon, Steve
Marron, Bonnie M.
Marsh, Tara
Marshall, Vivien
Masciantonio, Mike
Mayfield, Donald G.
McAfee, Julia
McBroom, Jan
McNutt, "Pete" (H.R.)
McNutt, Kathy
McNutt, Mildred
McNutt, Nancy Brentzel
Merenda, Jerry
Mertz, Doug
Meusel, Judy
Milburn, Janet M.
Miller, Sandra
Moore, Joanie
Morgan, Virginia J.
Morrison, Judy
Moyar, Joe
Mulcahy, Richard P.
Muller, Janet
Muller, Judy

Murphy, Thelma
Murray, Helen
Myers, Kathy
Nowlin, Ed
Nowlin, Sandy
Nowlin, Sue
Noyes, Robert P.

Padden, Fred
Patterson, Pat
Pedder, Charles
Perona, Joseph
Peterson, Mary Martha
Pietrusza, Phyllis
Piper, Paula J.
Plischke, John Jr.
Plischke, Dr. John
  (and his Jr. High Students)
Pollins, Calvin E.
Pollins, Frances J.
Pomputius, Mary Ann
Poole, Donald E.
Porter, William F.
Pringle, Bill
Pringle, Jonnie

Randolph, Debby
Ray, David
Ray, Robert
Raygor, Pam
Rebosky, Anita
Rebosky, Bill
Richards, Dick
Richardson, Dr. James
Riel, Donald
Roach, Lonny C.
Robertshaw, John

Sabo, Ethel
Schuck, Elizabeth
Seabury, Chris
Seabury, Jeff
Shaffer, Mark
Sloan, Armeda J.
Smith, Betsy (Elizabeth)
Smith, Cheryl Helene
Smith, Ed H.
Smith, Edward M.
Smith, Helene

Smith, Gregory
Smith, Jane
Smith, Jennifer
Smith, Laurel
Smith, Mary Jane
Smith, Michael
Smith, Shelley J.
Smith, W.R.
Sonnie, Scott
Spisso, Ronnie
Stoner, Joe
Street, Bruce
Swetnam, George

Tambly, Richard
Taylor, Jane
Taylor, William
Testa, Michael and Judy
Thomas, Gerald
Tobin, Bruce
Tobin, Doug
Treskovick, Barry
Truschel, Pat
Trusilo, Sharon M.

Van Atta, Robert B.
Vestrat, Glenn
Vestrat, Larry
Vogel, Eleanor

Warren, Ann, Arthur, and Kerry
W.A.S. Certification Class
Washlaski, Lee Bates
Washlaski, Mike
Washlaski, Ray
Weber, Dot
Welsh, Ian
Welshofer, Schon
Wesner, Molly
Westmoreland County Firemen
Williams, Jay G.
Wilson, Doug
Wilson, Helen
Wilson, Kirke

Yeager, Lisa A.
Yengst, Vickie
Yeoman, Mildred and Erica
Young, Dorothy
Yourish, Richard E.
Zorasak, Joan

CONTENTS

1 • DUST THOU ART

Deftly does the dust express
In mind her hidden loveliness,

. . . .

For the earth that breeds the trees
Breeds cities too, and symphonies.
JOHN HALL WHEELOCK

Reading the local newspaper is one of the standard pastimes in our outer-suburban homes. At this range every house has a hierarchy of at least four degrees in that respect. There is the metropolitan daily, designed for scanning the headlines and looking at the sports page; then the *Tribune Review*, printed seven days a week at the county seat; and the *Westmoreland Star*, in which we dutifully seek for news of the area.

But when it comes to the *Penn-Franklin*, our weekly township organ, printed right here in Murrysville (and don't put an "a" into the name unless you want to become a blood-feud enemy), duty calls. Every line is an obligation, which we must "read, mark, learn and mentally digest" as seriously as they used to do with the Apostles' Creed and Shorter Catechism when Grandpa was a boy.

If the custom isn't quite so unchangeable as the laws of the Medes and Persians, it at least is not to be lightly disregarded. We read the paper with care and in the end wrap up the garbage.

But surprise isn't customarily a part of the game. Usually we know already what has been or is going to happen. Until this appeared:

WANTED!

Enthusiastic and dedicated volunteers
to excavate and reconstruct historic
Revolutionary War-time village of Hanna's
Town, burned by Indians and British in 1782.

Duties may include digging up dirt with a
trowel and sifting it carefully. Workers
should expect no pay for the privilege of
putting in long hours of hard, slow work.

Were my eyes deceiving me? Did I read that ad incorrectly? As I read the words more carefully a second time, I knew that I had not been mistaken. But it was too good to be true—for here was a chance to do something I had yearned to do years ago and had all but forgotten.

Ever since I could remember I had wanted to excavate a historic site. What child does not grow up with some unfulfilled dream of adventure in a far-away land? Mine was to go to Egypt and dig among the pyramids and sphinxes along the Nile; hunt for Mayan ruins in Mexico; or follow Leakey throughout Africa. A preposterous obsession to be sure—especially now, since I have a husband and five school age children.

But perhaps part of my dream could come true, I thought. And I wouldn't have to make the long trip to Egypt, Mesopotamia, or even to the island of Bimini in pursuit of it.

Besides, by now our own local history had become more interesting to me than the romance of some far-off place. The opportunity sounded great, but the location was even more exciting. Why—I could practically dig in my own backyard, compared to the distance it would be to Egypt. For I *knew* where Hanna's Town was.

Oh, how well I knew Hanna's Town! It is a household word around here. There is a little golf course by that same name only a short distance from our home. Every week my husband beats a path out there to play. (There is no mistress quite like golf. No woman can compete with her!)

Golf is not a seasonal sport at our house—it goes on spring, summer, fall, and winter. Fair weather or foul, it is a constant activity. But Wayne is an excellent golfer—scoring in the low 70's—loves the game, and never gets upset if he has a bad day. And when a man does as well as that, such an ability should never be squelched. We pass this way but once, and he'll never have another chance if he doesn't enjoy life now.

"Why don't you take it up, too?" I am asked as a golf widow. When we were first married I did give it a try several times but found that meandering alone through the woods searching for an ornery white ball was not my cup or tee.

Personally, I think that it's great when a husband and wife share similar interests and pursue the same hobbies. But there has to be a sincere desire on both sides for it to be successful. It doesn't work if it is forced. One party gives in to the wishes of the other and becomes a martyr to the cause. Besides, too much togetherness sometimes causes bickering, nagging, and gnashing of teeth. Then you get to looking like one another, and what couple wants to be mistaken for twins?

As a result I am happy to say that we are still friends. And we don't look a bit alike. (After all, friendship *is* one of the most vital parts of love; for it is quite possible to love someone and treat that person like the enemy. It is unfortunate that in some cases familiarity does indeed breed contempt.)

I laid the paper aside and began to contemplate the possibility of becoming an amateur archeologist. Just as Wayne never insisted upon or expected me to play golf, I would certainly not make an issue of him coming along and digging with me. Besides, I don't think that he would "dig" it anyway, even if I were to make the request. But we could at least head in the same direction and be in close proximity. I had no idea where the historic Hanna's Town site was, but I surmised that it had to be somewhere close, since it had the same name as the golf course.

The more I thought about the idea the more exciting it became. But I knew that it would be an involvement other than just taking on another activity. For an undertaking such as this would surely require many hours of time. That word "dedicated . . ." from the ad kept echoing in my mind.

I cannot neglect my family, I told myself nobly. But on the other hand, the children are older now. After all, Wayne does play a lot of golf, I rationalized. And the days of diapers and kindergarten car pools were over as far as I was concerned. I had reached those years when women begin to feel no longer needed. A change had come over me and I began to seek a different kind of fulfillment, the kind Wayne seemed to get every time he came home refreshed and exhilarated from a game of golf. Women, too, must find a balance in life amid its confusion and activity. We need creative pauses and relationships more alive to ourselves and others in order to bring about inner, spiritual harmony.

Yet, how does one remain whole and balanced with all our multifarious distractions? In trying to do too much, we can throw ourselves off balance. In time we become drained and jaded. We need to renew the soul within by a more creative life pursuing our own interests. (We don't have to force contentment sitting next to our spouses while feigning interest in a football or baseball game.)

Women want to be considered as whole persons, not as collections of functions. Most of the physical and time-consuming work has disappeared from homemaking today, but along with it has gone much of the creative aspect as well. Perhaps this is why there is an upsurge of attention given to former necessities which today we call early American arts and crafts—a need which the distaff is beginning to feel more than ever before.

Was I alone or were there many more like me in households across the nation, pondering the same thing? Maybe I did need to get out and broaden my interests—like a child when all his "mirrors become windows" and he begins to see with farther vision—the earth—and others, like himself—personal fulfillment, hopes, dreams. There is an exciting world out there—somewhere beyond dishpans, dirty laundry, and TV. My mind was about to erupt, I thought, motivated with ambition and a new awakening. And I began to yearn even more for that certain intangible something beyond the call of duty at home.

But on the other side of the coin, the house just couldn't get along without my constant cleaning and supervision, I reflected in all modesty. No, I just can't take the time for volunteer archeology. Or could I?

And so, contrary to my logical reasoning, the matter was decided. I would go and dig! Who knows? This new adventure of mine may interest some of the young hopefuls and give them an outlet, too, I reasoned. They may even want to come along and help.

One thing was in my favor: at least I was not involved in women's clubs, leagues, circles, squares and what have you. Years ago I had already gone down that road—so to speak—and now needed a breath of fresh air. Or perhaps it was the inherent Viking blood in me that would not permit confinement to the indoors for very long at a time. In either case I wouldn't be shackled by numerous meetings to attend.

My thoughts were busy weighing the possibilities of how I could budget my time better. Between raising a family and keeping house, it was hard to squeeze anything more into the hours of the day. Something would have to go if I were to indulge in archeology. But what?

As it turned out, I did relinquish something—an activity that most women would like to forget about altogether—being a housewife. (I use the term loosely and with distaste. How I abhor that word! For one thing it sounds too much on the same parallel with house dog or house cat. And the word itself usually conjures up the stereotype of a woman with a scarf tied around her head and a wet mop in one hand. Language powerfully shapes our thoughts and attitudes! Besides, whoever heard of engineer husband, office husband, truck driver husband, doctor husband, or even *househusband* (how the men would cringe!) or whatever the case may be? Does the word necessarily have to designate where the person is likely to be or what the occupation is? Today the word is obsolete, for women no longer spend all their time in the house making apple butter, quilting, weaving, spinning wool. What is wrong with the term wife—the equivalent of husband?)

And so being a wife, one soon learns the secret of dust and its mystic qualities. When you run a cloth over a piece of furniture, a good percentage of the particles are dispersed into the air only to come right back down again at another time, rearranged but just as thick. "Dust thou art and dust thou dost return." If I do decide to take the time out during the day to dig, who is to know whether I have lifted the dust once a week, twice a week, or seven times? And I will have accomplished so very much in the meantime.

Come what may, that's what I shall do. I took a deep breath, and like the heroine in an old-fashioned dime novel, straightened up to my fullest height. I will surrender my former traditional habits, I told myself bravely, as if it were a great sacrifice. I would take an accelerated, more positive approach by not putting off today what can be done tomorrow. In this new blitz method of housekeeping I decided to become better organized.

I will get into the habit of never entering a room unless I improve it in some way or another. If something is out of place—pick it up. If dirty—clean it. Why delay until spring house cleaning? (Whatever that is anyway—probably a hangover from the past when our ancestors had to wait for the spring thaw before they could beat their rugs and air the feathers in their ticks.)

No longer would there be time for wasted motion. Just as Benjamin Franklin once said years ago: "Dost thou love life, then do not squander time, for that's the stuff life is made of. Lost time is never found again." And I'm inclined to go along with Ben in this respect. After all, I only have so long to live. But what I'm saying is true of us all. Our lives are like dandelions whose blossoms are yellow for a brief time, and then in transparency disappear with the wind. So why not make the most of every moment that we have?

In the process of saving time, the house may not be as perfect as it could be, but in the words of the English philosopher, Herbert Spencer, laying special emphasis on happiness and personal development: "The primary use of work is that of supplying the materials and aids to living completely . . . any other uses are secondary." Besides, when I die I know that no one is going to inscribe, "She was a most meticulous housekeeper," on my tombstone—not even if I had been one. They'll more likely write, "She's done—but her housework ain't!"

That night when Wayne came home for dinner, I excitedly

asked him, "Where's Hanna's Town?" He looked at me in a most peculiar manner, as if I had suddenly lost my mind.

"Where—is—Hanna's Town?" he repeated in a slow puzzled voice. "You've gotta be kidding!"

I said, "I mean historic Hanna's Town," and I showed him the ad.

"Oh, I know where that is," he said taking the newspaper. "That's just a mile or so down the road from the golf course. It's the Steel property now. Better known as the Hanna's Town Courthouse Farm. Want to take a ride out tonight to see it?"

I thought he would never ask!

2 • COUNTRY ROADS

Where did it come from, where did it go?
That was the question that puzzled me so
As we waded the dust of the highway that flowed
By the farm, like a river—the old country road.

JAMES NEWTON MATTHEWS

It was a glorious Indian summer day when I turned off the busy, hectic highway at Harvey's Five Points crossing, and onto a quiet country road. And I thought of the words written by Emily Dickinson:

These are the days when skies put on
The old, old sophistries of June,
A blue and gold mistake.

It had been less than a week ago that I made my first journey along this scenic route with Wayne and the children.

According to legend, a blockhouse stood on the high hill overlooking the crossroads two hundred years ago. Whether true or not, from this secluded location you can see one of the most magnificent views imaginable.

To the settlers back in the time of Hanna's Town, a blockhouse was a necessity, for Pennsylvania had no military then and was powerless to resist the numerous Indian attacks, which resulted from the white man's continuing encroachments.

There was always a sudden chill of horror when Indian summer was mentioned, let alone when it arrived. Today we regretfully watch the birds fly southward as days grow shorter with the oncoming winter. Years ago warm weather was hailed dubiously, for throughout spring and early fall the pioneers were cooped up in forts and blockhouses. This was the time that Indians were most likely to attack. And when the weather stayed nice on into the fall, the settlers would live in fear of the extended season.

Thus, winter was a safer period for them. We look forward to spring with great anticipation, but the settlers knew that the Indians would be stirred up again with its onset; and to make matters worse, it was the tradition for the first prisoner taken each spring to be burned at the stake. Now as I reached the top of the next hill I thanked my lucky stars that my family and I were living through the Indian summers of the twentieth century—and not back in the "good old days."

I looked across the rolling hills of green and late summer amber. A patchwork of varicolored fields lay on both sides of the road, interrupted only by clumps of trees and an occasional house or two. Along the way a few stalks of late blooming chicory could still be seen. Fresh breezes and open countryside. Such was the course that I was destined to take, not only this day, but many, many times to come. Taking my everyday blinders off, I began to see for the first time the world that had always been around me. My mind was awakening from a humdrum sleep. I began to come alive again. Suddenly there was space for beauty and significance in life. And I sensed for the first time a spirit of peace and freedom that I would in the future look forward to whenever I came this way.

The road was no ordinary one. I knew it well and was familiar with the landmarks that led to Hanna's Town. General John Forbes had directed the building of the road for military purposes in 1758. His forces blazed the way from Raystown (now Bedford) to Fort Duquesne (later Fort Pitt) where they captured the fortress and expelled the French from their strategic stronghold. Soon I came to the little village of Forbes Road, a constant reminder that the general's troops had passed this way before our time.

Suddenly a mother pheasant and her brood darted out of the brush into the road in front of me. No one was coming in either direction and I was able to dodge, missing them by only a few feet. This was something that the settlers of Hanna's Town were not familiar with, I mused, for this bird was not introduced to America until whalers and silk merchants first imported them from China.

The original ones in Pennsylvania were brought by private individuals in 1850. When our forefathers said "pheasant," they meant the ruffed grouse—or sometimes the ivory billed woodpecker, now extinct. I wondered what other animals Forbes' men must have encountered when they made the wilderness road and marched here. No doubt many wild turkeys, deer, and squirrels scampered out of their way, along with stealthy panthers (same as western mountain lions) and bears plodding through the dark woods.

A few more bends in the road took me past the location of three military redoubts that were built by George Washington's men as they marched with Forbes. There was nothing there now except a grassy flat point of land looking out over the valley below where black and white Holstein cows munched peacefully on the grass. Who would have guessed that thousands of men had once camped here for several nights? All the eye could detect now was an autumn landscape.

On the map I had noticed Crabtree Creek meandering through this land, not far from here. I could see mute evidence of the name in the small trees lining the roadside, laden with their fall harvest. And, I thought, even if there were no points of interest along this road, it was still a very pleasant ride.

Just then the radio began to play "Country Roads," and my foot pressed on the gas pedal a little harder than necessary. "Slow down," I told myself. "You'll get there soon enough."

Farther on, after the road had almost made a horseshoe curve, was a small cemetery on the right. It was so small that there were only nine moss-covered headstones protruding from the ground. Around the somber cluster was a split rail fence. The grass within its confines was mowed and well kept. But beyond lay a thick, wild blackberry patch. I wondered if there had been other stones. Where were all the early settlers of Hanna's Town buried? The epitaphs of those

I could discern had flaked off the markers. Other stones had crumbled one by one, leaving only a few remaining to stand the elements of time.

> Beneath those rugged elms, that yew tree's shade,
>> Where heaves the turf in many a mouldering heap,
> Each in his narrow cell for ever laid,
>> The rude Forefathers of the hamlet sleep.

How true those words of Thomas Gray seemed now. I passed on by, eager to get to my destination.

On the left side of the road, just a short distance from the early burial ground, was a larger private graveyard. A tall obelisk in the center marked the Steel cemetery—the last of the original land still possessed by that family within the historic site. I had been told that all the 173 acres now owned by the county since 1969 had been purchased by the Steels in 1826 and remained in their hands until recently—one family being the sole heirs of this property all that time. Fortunately so, for the land was unspoiled and saved from prospective developers who would have ruined any possible chance of restoration.

A whitewashed fence completely surrounded the cemetery at the top of the hill. Beyond it in a valley lay the site of old Hanna's Town. A chill went through me. I had seen the spot before, I recalled. But this time I had come to help dig up its long forgotten past.

3 • THE DESERTED VILLAGE

Sweet smiling village, loveliest of the lawn,
Thy sports are fled, and all thy charms withdrawn;

. . . .

Sunk are thy bowers in shapeless ruin all,
And the long grass o'ertops the mouldering wall . . .

OLIVER GOLDSMITH

A site for sore eyes! I looked down from the hill and saw my destination nestled in a fertile green valley that had become farmland ever since the burning of Hanna's Town on that fateful thirteenth day of July in 1782. Laurel and Chestnut Ridges, bluish gray foothills of the great Alleghenies, lay beyond.

At the base of the hill was a comfortable-looking farmhouse, and just east of it on the same side of the Forbes Road was a huge white barn. I turned into the driveway and parked my car near it. A flock of gray pigeons fluttered from its rafters as I approached. Looking up, I saw high above my head the words, "Hanna's Town Courthouse Farm" written on the front in large bold letters. By its weathered boards and chipped paint, I could tell that this barn must have been a familiar landmark for many years.

In the very center of the yard, between the house and the barn, was a small stone structure which enclosed a fresh-running spring. Secured to the large roof support was a bronze plaque. I walked over to see what it said and read the words:

Site of Hanna's Town Fort
1774
Marked by Phoebe Bayard Chapter
D.A.R.
Greensburg, Pa. 1913

At the time I had no idea who Phoebe Bayard was, but with a little research I discovered that she was Brigadier General Arthur St. Clair's wife. He was one of the leaders in forming Westmoreland County and was elected president of the Continental Congress in 1787. In time he was chosen Governor of the Northwest Territory, which included all the land west of Pennsylvania and Virginia, and north of the Ohio River.

Close by was another, somewhat larger structure—a one-time root cellar—which was partially underneath the ground. This edifice later was to become the first field museum on the site.

Below these two was a third building where the water from the first spring flowed underneath into three consecutive troughs at a lower level. I soon learned that this milk house, or springhouse as it was commonly called, is a good place to cool off on a hot summer's day. The water was always ice-cold. And splashing it on one's self provided instant relief after working in the hot, scorching sun.

Looking toward the east I could see the crossroads and a little log and frame house. It was weather-beaten and appeared as if it had stood many a storm. Now as I turned south and looked beyond the road I could see an enormous field stretching out before me, without any buildings or trees to obstruct the view. And I wondered what used to be there. Perhaps some day I would find out.

Just then I heard a muffled sound to the west of the house and barn behind me. A short distance away, the ground was marked off with stakes into squares—and down in the center of one which had been excavated, a young woman with long reddish-blond hair was kneeling. She had a trowel in her hand and was scraping the dirt toward her. I walked over and struck up a conversation. Very soon I discovered that we had something in common—a mutual interest in Hanna's Town.

When I introduced myself to her she said:

"Just call me Mary Jane."

She had scooped up the loose dirt and had placed it on a large screen that was resting on top of a wheelbarrow. I watched her push the soil to and fro as she searched for hidden artifacts. Mary Jane looked for any material remains of man—his weapons and tools, what he had made and used, and even bones or other evidence of the foods he had eaten. But moving in a little closer for a better look, all I could see were stones and dirt.

Back and forth her hand moved until at last it stopped and she picked up a ceramic fragment. She showed it to me before placing it in a brown paper bag. To me it appeared to be nothing more than just a piece of a broken dish. But there was more to it than that. She was able to tell exactly what it was. From its brilliant, shiny surface, hard inner white paste or body, and flecks of black, she could classify it as a shard of ironstone, dating no earlier than the beginning of the nineteenth century, when this type of earthenware was first manufactured.

I felt elated. Already I had learned something.

"Doggone it!" Mary Jane exclaimed in sudden dismay.

I looked at her with surprise. "I think that's a nice find," I said with an inexperienced eye.

"Not at this level," she complained. "I'm down fourteen inches, right where this layer indicates that it should be from the Hanna's Town period and this late piece of white ware shows up. How did it get here, among all these other artifacts from the 1700s? Things sure have a way of getting mixed up."

I hadn't thought about that before. But the good terra is not selective about the secrets it reveals. And man has a way of not only changing its surface from time to time but also mixing everything in it as well, like egg beaters of the earth. Each time a farmer tills his field in the spring he changes the location of artifacts—some up and others down—breaking them even more and dispersing them throughout the plow zone.

Sometimes pits for dumping rubbish are dug next to or are

overlapping those of an earlier era, only adding to the frustration of the archeologist and making it difficult to interpret the finds.

For example, one of the inhabitants of Hanna's Town may have dug a pit for his trash, and a farmer of a later period may dig one to bury an animal. The newer pit may introduce objects of its own time into the level of the earlier one. And unless this disturbance is identified, there will be confusion.

It is interesting to predict the future of archeology in this respect. For some day when humankind becomes involved in excavating the artifacts of our era, it will be even more difficult than it is now. Our customs have changed, and so must archeology in years to come.

Today refuse is not thrown down the little houses of necessity that once graced back yards, or in abandoned wells as it was in the past. Neither is it buried in deposits near our dwelling places. Instead it is hauled miles away in trucks to locations where everyone's trash is mingled in one common area or burned in incinerators, losing all identity as to the original owners and from whence it came.

"You must have had a course in archeology or studied it in school at one time?" I commented.

"No, I never have," Mary Jane admitted. "But my husband and I have been interested in this site for a good many years. We've known the history of the locality and have just been itching to come out here to dig. Then when the county bought the land for restoration and archeological excavations, we joined the Westmoreland Historical Society and were here when the project began."

She told me that they had dug a trial trench while searching for evidence of concentrated occupation and came upon a midden or rubbish pit—a gold mine to archeologists— soon after the ground was broken. Here many artifacts such as buckles, buttons, knives, two-tined forks, bone combs, watch keys, brass spigots, enamel twist wine glass stems, rum bottle shards, clay pipes, pewter ware, and jews harps had turned up. Along with land deeds and evidence of early charred logs, these finds showed where the courthouse-tavern had probably stood.

"That must have been quite a find," I murmured.

"Yes," she agreed. "Especially since this was the meeting place for the first English courts west of the Allegheny Mountains.

"One of the custom laws at that time was that a man could beat his wife, provided the stick was no thicker than the judge's thumb. And here were the pillory, jailhouse, and stocks—the lower rungs of split-rail fences were used when more stocks were needed. Along with these, the courthouse-tavern insured that there would be law and order."

"Isn't that rather an unusual place to hold court—in a tavern?" I asked. "What havoc there must have been!"

"Yes," Mary Jane replied. "To us it seems strange. But you must remember that in those days there were few schools, churches, and no community centers or other public buildings on the frontier where people could meet to discuss their problems. The taverns became the hubs of most social activities. They were our first insurance offices, and traveling parsons even preached in their barrooms.

"At that time the county of Bedford was so vast that it was difficult for people in this territory to travel that distance across the mountains, to take care of legal matters," she went on. "So in 1773 a new county, by the name of Westmoreland—named after one in England—was formed, and it included about a fourth of the state of Pennsylvania."

I remembered the words of Frank Cowan, Westmoreland's eccentric genius of a century ago:

> The Little World was a wild, wild wood,
>   Without or shape or laws,
> When George the Third declared the word,
>   And Lo! Westmoreland was!

"To us, that still seems like a large territory," said Mary Jane. "But at least it was more convenient than before.

"Previous to this time a north-county Irishman by the name of Robert Hanna had taken up land and built a log house beside the Forbes Road, which for years carried most of the overland traffic to Pittsburgh. He and his wife, Elizabeth, began to keep a tavern here; and this proved to be so successful that the area, which was originally known as Myer's spring, became Hanna's Town, in his honor. Hanna's inn was chosen as the meeting house for the county to hold court."

I tried to imagine how that tap house might have looked at one time:

> It stands all alone like a goblin in gray,
> The old-fashioned inn of a pioneer day,
> In a land so forlorn and forgotten, it seems
> Like a wraith of the past rising into our dreams;
> Its glories have vanished, and only the ghost
> Of a sign-board now creaks on its desolate post,
> Recalling a time when all hearts were akin
> As they rested a night in that welcoming inn.

As the words of James Matthews echoed in my mind, I suddenly wished that the voices of the past could somehow be heard. It seems that all things change except human nature. Surely these people who lived in Hanna's Town years ago and those from time immemorial, had the same emotions and feelings that we know today—with a few modifications of words and expressions.

My imagination began to run away with me. All of a sudden I fancied myself as Elizabeth Hanna, the innkeeper's wife. Such are the dimensions of the mind . . .

* * * * * * * *

Aye, "jocund day stands tiptoe on the misty mountain-top" T'would be a joy to sleep late some morning. And especially this morning after all the vociferous merriment that went on last night. (Ach, drat those pesky beasts! If only we could escape from these fleas and bugs.)

Such an evening . . more guests than we knew what to do with. All those men of savage appearance and outlandish dress. An over-abundance of Frenchmen and others, many of them flitters, to be sure . . each wanting accommodation. And that set of hunters who put up for the night here. What a pair they turned out to be!

The whole group was rowdy. It's a good thing that I was able to get them interested in husking some corn. At least that seemed to keep them busy for a while . . that is until the one hunter started to take a fancy to Jeanette. And come to think of it, after the chores were finished, he seemed quite willing to fetch more wood to keep a cheerful fire burning on the hearth. Ah, I can still see the glow of that fire as he danced to the fiddle—roaring with laughter. It brought back so many memories.

Jeanette seemed to like him. How jovial he became as evening drew to a close. While all the time that other one sat in the chimney corner smoking his pipe—that is, when he wasn't engaged in his favorite pastime of whistling.

I wonder what it was that caused all the fracas when everyone joined in the frolic. Such a scene of bacchanalia! Something must surely have provoked the chap to start that whirlwind of a fight. I would have preferred his constant whistling, to the brawl that took place. Perhaps it was over a political argument . . or . . I must speak to Jeanette when she awakens. I had begun to fear for our personal safety until that fine preacher from Philadelphia appeared. He seemed to come out of the shadows from nowhere. And the way he addressed those two hunters on the indecorum of fighting in the presence of ladies. How elegantly he spoke. I shall long remember his words: "Intoxication, though excusable in a gentleman, is by no means an apology for a breach of the laws of good breeding; and the respect which every man feels himself bound, in honor and in duty, to pay to the female sex." I haven't heard anyone speak so gallant in a long time.

It was a good thing that we ran out of whiskey—or at least that's what Robert told our unruly guests. And then when that one saucy fop tried to extirpate our signpost—well, I'm glad now that I threatened to have them both locked up in the jail house or put in the stocks and pillory. They had no right to complain!

Oh well, at least I can hear by all the snoring around that they're still asleep. Now if I can just crawl over Robert and try not to awaken the girls. And wind my way through all the rest of the forms rolled up in their bedclothes. It is so difficult to make everyone comfortable when there are never enough bedsteads, and when those that we have are overflowing, with the rest of the guests sleeping on the floor. Thank goodness court isn't held every day, or I should soon lose my mind . . along with my sanity.

At least I have some privacy to get dressed. Those poor women guests in the other room have none. And some men are like beasts, when a woman's around. But that parson from Philadelphia . . . well, I must not tarry.

How dreadfully cold it is this morning! I detest the very thought of stepping out into this bedchamber where the crisp air goes right through one. I wonder if some day, there will ever be a means to keep a house warm all during the night and into the morning without having to get up and throw a pine log onto the fire every hour. Wouldn't it be splendid to remain warm and comfortable all the while, instead of roasting on one side and freezing on the other, in front of the fire. But I don't suppose that day will ever come—at least not in my time.

Now to forget the cold and start breakfast before our guests are up and moving about. I think that it would be prudent to prepare as many victuals as our larder will provide, since we ran out of certain spirituous liquor last evening. We must uphold our reputation for an excellent fare, whatever we do.

Perhaps breakfast of corn meal mush, honey, dried berries, bread, apple butter, and fried bear left over from last night would put them all in a good mood to start the day—since it is so important with court in session. Better not serve any squirrel. Some have been complaining about too much of that lately. It's so difficult to please everyone.

Oh dear, that sign on the wall keeps reminding me about our needs. It seems to stand out even more at times like this:

"*Whiskey*—four pence per gill; *strong beer*—eight pence per quart; *cider*—one shilling per quart."

How can a tavern expect to make money with the court regulating prices like that?

What's that I hear outside? I can't seem to make out the distorted figures through this green window glass, and the misty morning doesn't help much either. I wish it were our supplies, but I'm afraid it is not. Could it be military agents? There's too many for it to be the express. Perhaps it's early arrivals for court, wanting to trade furs.

Oh no! Not another Indian deputation from Pittsburgh, and

of all days! At least I hear Robert up now. Mercy, it didn't take those Indians long to get off their horses and knock at the door. It sounds like they're going to break it in. Something must surely have aroused them. Have they no patience? Better unbar the door quick. Don't want to get them any angrier than they seem.

"I'm coming, I'm coming!"

My goodness, there are so many. Well, Robert can appease them. It looks like that big one is going to do all the talking. Sounds as if they've been cheated by some white men at the last trading post. Oh dear, now they want whiskey and our supply is out.

"But can't you understand—we have none. Hath you no ears?"

My God, he's coming toward me with a raised tomahawk!

* * * * * * *

Mary Jane was still moving the dirt around in her screen. When I hadn't spoken for a while, she looked up and asked:

"Would you like to help? If you really are interested you must work along with an experienced volunteer until you know enough about it to be on your own."

I was still in a daze, but then remembering why I was there, I immediately placed my hand in the warm earth and felt the pulse of time. I began what was to be an exciting new adventure—that day and every day since.

If I thought an object looked like something other than a stone, I questioned Mary Jane, and was repaid with a word of practical wisdom.

"When in doubt, it's best to put it in the bag. Cleaning it later may help determine if it should be saved or not. You can always throw it away at that time, but if you pass an object up there's no telling whether it will ever be found again."

My first season at the site ended with more bags of meaningless stones and other debris than anything else. But it takes that experience the first year for one's eyes to become accustomed to seeing what really is in the soil and what one should be looking for.

Learning to recognize irregular, rusty bits of metal that can be taken for stones; bone that after being in the ground for some time resembles smooth, dark wood: and tiny green copper straight pins that can be mistaken for grass and easily missed, is an important step to the student of archeology.

To be suspicious of triangular pieces of matter, which could be cut segments of a coin (that was how our forefathers made change); to tell the difference between red dog and redware (in case you've never lived in the coal mining country, red dog is burned refuse from a mine dump.) We save the "ware" but not the "dog"; to distinguish rectangular bits and pieces of lead (the first step in the evolution of pencils) from stone particles.

To differentiate between pebbles and musket or rifle balls, and to tell a piece of glass from a particle of slate—it all sounds easy. But with the sun shining on these items which are covered with dirt, they are sometimes hard to identify. However, there are ways. For instance, holding an object up to the sunlight will soon tell you whether or not it is glass. And the weight of a bullet is certainly more than that of a pebble. But I was unaware of this fact until I started digging at Hanna's Town. (At first I thought that I was the only female ignorant about such matters, until one day two women came to the site and asked me: "How can you tell when you've found a musket ball?" And I brilliantly told them!)

These are just a few examples of the many "look-alikes" that tend to confuse the eye from time to time.

The day had gone faster than I anticipated, and soon it was time to go home. Mary Jane walked over to the car with me. In the course of our conversation she told me more about what Hanna's Town was like in the 1700s. Here had been a village of about thirty log houses and a fort, in addition to the renowned Hanna's courthouse-tavern. There were other taverns here, too, and of course the much-needed blacksmith shop. A far-away look came into her eyes.

"Somewhere out there," she said sweeping her arm in front of her, "were streets which we know were called Penn, Thompson, Strawberry Alley, and Front—or Main—on the Forbes Road . . ."

All of a sudden the site began to come alive once more. For a moment I saw a busy, bustling town. Real people lived on streets just as we do. And I know that many a tear must have fallen here, by the same token that made sure laughter had once echoed from the hillside nearby. These people had sown the surrounding fields each spring, and harvested them every autumn. They had drunk cool water from the same fresh running stream that to this day flows from the earth. They had toiled here, and loved here, and had eked out a living from this very soil. They, too, had experienced frustrations, grief, and worries, along with their hopes and dreams. Happiness was theirs, here, on this land. The more I thought about it, the more I wanted to get involved.

What a hobby, I thought! Sunshine and fresh air. No cumbersome equipment to buy, store, or carry around from place to place; no boat, no motor, no surfboards; no skiis, poles or special shoes; no caddy fees and not even a bag of clubs, balls, and tees. Only an old pair of gloves. This was for me!

4 • TROWELS AND TRIBULATIONS

*No man is born into the world whose work
Is not born with him; there is always work . . .*
JAMES RUSSELL LOWELL

Where and how does one begin, I wondered? This was the first day that I was on my own at Hanna's Town. It was all new to me, and never having had a course in archeology, I felt very uneasy about the whole thing.

My mind quickly recalled sun-filled days of my early youth. I could see myself and others hunting through the debris of forgotten bonfires and poking about with a stick for hidden treasures. At that time it was the custom to burn all the trash in a certain place near the back of one's yard—the pre-pollution, conscious era. And we had an alley running past our property with such interesting spots you would not believe.

One could always find pretty perfume bottles that had melted and turned all the colors of the rainbow from the heat of the fire; broken pottery; blobs and globs of molten glass in any shape or shade; or if lucky, even a coin that had been thrown out by mistake. That was my first and only experience at digging. And if early impressions are important, perhaps it predisposed me in the direction that I was taking today. But now I was about to work in a more methodical way, finding and saving artifacts—not for myself, who in time would only lose them along with their meaning—but for some permanent museum. (In fact, after you have worked at a professional dig you no longer have the desire to take home the artifacts. Instead you come home with a sense of having participated not only in scientific research, but in adventure as well.) Suddenly it all seemed worthwhile.

This time the director of archeology was there—a handsome, good-natured man whom we all liked and knew as Jake. He pointed to the ground, showing me the area that was to be mine to dig.

"The site is staked out by a grid system of 50-foot squares resembling a checkerboard," he said. "These are then subdivided into sixteen 10-foot squares which are separated by 2-foot balks." (Yes, it will audit if you don't forget there are balks at the sides, too.)

Forget the details, I said to myself. Just let me begin! I looked at the grass-covered area marked off with four stakes and was anxious to get started.

"I'm assigning you this 5-foot square, which is a fourth of a 10-foot section. We work on one quarter at a time. The balks should not be excavated until all 10-foot squares in the region of exploration are dug," he went on.

"Now, what all do I save?" I asked impatiently.

"All items made or used by man. New or old," he replied. "Your bag should include the following information: Site Name, Level, Number of Square, Date, Your own Name, and Comments. Write it on the side for easy reference."

As Jake handed me a bag, he emphasized how important it was to have all this written down, for by its nature archeology is a destructive science.

"Any excavating, no matter how well it is done, is a waste of time and is meaningless disruption unless it is recorded as accurately as possible," he told me. "Careless digging can ruin a feature."

I was not sure of what he meant by this statement, and when Jake saw my puzzled expression, he continued:

"A feature is any man-made disturbance in the soil that can be isolated. For example—refuse pits, foundations, charred logs, fire pits and post-molds (which become post-holes after they are excavated). Most of our information comes from features, and beginners should not attempt to remove them," he said. "Stones and charred logs should remain in place until drawings and photographs are taken."

I began to get nervous, just thinking about all the disruption and destruction that I was capable of doing.

He went on, oblivious to my inner turmoil.

"Generally we dig in 6-inch levels. For example 0" to 6", 6" to 12", 12" to 18". However, this may vary. Modern fill areas may be removed as one level, and standard 6-inch levels should not be used if color changes are observed in the soil."

Taking a trowel in his hand and scraping with it, Jake said: "Color changes can only be observed if *thin* layers of earth are removed. Allowing the square to be covered with loose dirt or attempting to remove 3 to 6-inch layers at one time will obscure or destroy color changes and features may be overlooked."

I began to wonder if I should be here at all. And when he said: "In addition to information needed on the bag, an archeological summary report form should be filled out for each square," I almost turned and ran. But for some reason, I stayed there, glued to the spot, asking more questions.

"What do I do with the bags?" I said weakly.

"You are required to clean, gently but thoroughly, what you find. Ceramics and glass are washed with nothing but water, and metal is brushed lightly to dislodge the dirt. Do not attempt to remove rust from metals. Allow them to dry completely, so that further corrosion does not occur.

"On the other hand, wood and leather must be stored in plastic bags to keep them damp. By the way, moisture is important when charred logs are exposed, too. They are sprinkled with water frequently to keep them from crumbling and flaking because of exposure to the air.

"After the artifacts are cleaned," Jake continued, "they are sorted, counted, numbered, and catalogued. And eventually a permanent identification mark will be placed on each specimen so that there is no possibility of important data being lost. Good records are even more valuable than artifacts.

"Place glass, ceramics, iron, chinking, and other items in separate containers after they have been counted, and label each bag as to where they were found and at what level," he said.

"If you use plastic bags, don't seal them tightly. Trapped moisture will promote mold growth which would destroy the information on the labels inside. Place the processed materials in the original bag and return them to the site," Jake went on.

"As many as possible will then be repaired and restored for preservation in the museum. It is like working on an endless puzzle. And we sometimes have to act like detectives trying to fit clues together in solving a case."

While I stood there in fear of what he would say next, Jake added: "Our primary objective in doing this is to locate structures related to the 1773-1786 period—when Hanna's Town was the County seat—for purposes of reconstruction."

I still can't understand how Hanna's Town acquired this honor way out here," I interrupted, looking across the undeveloped countryside.

"Well, with a newly formed county, the residents had to decide on a location for a county seat," explained Jake. "In those early days the only flourishing places in the territory were Pittsburgh and Hanna's Town. And both villages began to vie for the title and honor. There were those who wanted it to be in Pittsburgh, saying in support of their argument that Hanna's Town would not be practical. Where would one hold court there? The only house of any size was Hanna's tavern. These men argued that there would not be room enough at the inn or a sufficient number of chairs. If the building became overcrowded, the justices, magistrates, and all those attending court would have to meet out under a tree with their papers blowing away or getting wet during foul weather. Besides, at that time Pittsburgh even had a fort, while the one here wasn't built until a year after the county was organized.

"But Hanna must have been a leader of men, in addition to the fact that this place was most centrally located," Jake continued. "For he and a friend, Joseph Erwin, along with a few others, had enough political pull; thus Hanna's Town became the first county seat with his tavern as the courthouse. That is, until a suitable one could be built. And as politics go, something like that could be delayed as long as those who are influential are in power," said Jake with a wink.

"By the way, Robert Hanna died in 1786 and shortly afterward, a courthouse *was* built—but not in Hanna's Town. The second and present county seat was moved to Newtown, about three miles away. Today we know it as Greensburg.

"At any rate, this is where court met for a dozen years, at least, and since there were no shops as we know of them today—there being only a few stores—Hanna's tavern became a convenient place to get such commodities as gunpowder, lead, camphor and spices, thimbles, dye stuffs, jews harps, and jackknives—along with liquid refreshment."

Once again I began to imagine what it was like at this busy courthouse-tavern. At one time it must have bustled with activity—people coming and going—trading whiskey, corn, hides, salt, flour, bacon, and linen.

"The first court was held here on April 6, 1773," Jake went on. "And Colonel William Crawford was on the bench for that session as the presiding justice."

I remembered this story well. Colonel Crawford—scout, soldier, Indian fighter, confidant and friend of George Washington—contributed much in forging United States history. Unfortunately he was burned at the stake in 1782 by Delawares who blamed him for someone else's killing many Christian Indians at the Moravian villages on the Muskingum in Ohio—just a month before Hanna's Town was burned. Some people in more recent years had even conjectured that Hanna's Town was attacked in retaliation for what he allegedly had done. How uncertain the fate of humans, I pondered. I could sense a presence of a ghost of the departed past. I tried to put myself in his place . . .

* * * * * * * *

What a miserable day this is for our first court. Of all times for it to rain in the county-town. How unlike yesterday—a beautiful spring afternoon. Leaves just starting to come out on trees—and trailing arbutus with blossoms half-hidden in the tangle of dried foliage and vines left from last winter.

Now this drizzling rain, with mud weighting down the

horses' feet, and wagons hardly able to move through the mire. The crowd's already great. I wonder how they can make it through these impossible ruts of clay to this God-forsaken town. How Hanna was able to convince them to have the county seat here, is beyond me.

Mustn't forget to purchase some camphor and spices at Hanna's. Better pick up a good jackknife, too.

"Oh, good morning Robert—if you can call it that. Looks like it's going to rain all day, from the appearance of those clouds. Ready for our first session? The crowd's getting restless. Perhaps we had best get started. I'm afraid that foul weather and hordes of people do not make good bed-fellows . . .

"Shall we proceed with the business at hand . . . Order! . . Let there be order in this . . . ahem, courtroom. We shall now commence with the division of our new county into townships . . ."

What an ordeal! I thought they would never decide on those boundary lines. Began to think it was going to go on all day, like the rain. That Hanna can be stubborn as an ox at times. Thought he'd never agree on a satisfactory line for Hempfield Township. Well, at last that matter is finished. What I need now is a good drink.

"Ah, my pretty miss. I would be most happy if you would bring me a drink of the finest whiskey you have in the house. I've had a trying day."

A voluptuous delight to be sure! All that hair of flame and skin like silk. What a kitten she would be like to take . . .

"Oh, thank you my love. Now don't worry your pretty head over that. You needn't apologize to me, my sweet. No one should ever cry over a little spilt whiskey."

A real beauty, but somewhat clumsy, I must say.

"Aye, Robert. There you are. Sit right down and take a load off your feet. You have enough capable barmaids—ahem. Besides we all need to relax after a session like that.

"Here comes Arthur Sinclair* through the crowd. Now, lass, would you be so kind as to fetch us two more noggins

*St. Clair

of—make it some of that West India rum this time—the best you have. And mind—with care.

"Well, what do you think, men? Do you feel that the citizens of Westmoreland County are satisfied with their eleven new townships? Personally I think that we have done well, considering the boisterous crowd, lack of chairs and half of the townspeople exposed to the elements. Yes, I am well pleased and happy to know that we have accomplished so much on this eventful day, gentlemen . . .

* * * * * * * *

Where has the time gone? Nine years ago, and it only seems like yesterday when I was proudly standing before the residents of our county. And now—naked and painted black, tied to a stake like an animal, being slowly roasted! Where is the law and order now—the justice?

"Girty, for God's sake get your rifle and put an end to me. Take me out of my misery!"

Ruthless devil! I expect these savages to act this way, but a white man whom I could have called friend? He sits there and laughs, after what he has seen me go through. His heart must be stone.

My eyes, my eyes. They are ready to burst. Although the sight is gone from me, I can see even more clearly those red-hot, burning coals they force me to walk on. Oh God, how much can one man endure? Is there no end to this torment? How can men torture one another so fiendishly?

I cannot bear this excruciating pain much longer. If only Simon Girty would shoot me and release my body from this brutality. I had no idea what hell was really like until now.

What more can they do to me? "I didn't do it. I didn't murder your women and children. I . . ."

My strength is almost gone. How many hours has it been? Is it yet dawn? I'm losing my senses . . . am so weak. Feels as if they're using my own jackknife on me now. Or is it the burning firebrands again?

Oh God, not that! All my life I have lived in fear of being scalped at the hands of savages. Have mercy on my soul. Not more burning coals . . . on my raw scalp. The noise of their demoniac yelling . . . it's all starting to fade now.

I had known such happiness. Life was so blithe. I loved justice and hated iniquity . . . and now must die unjustly. I no longer feel the pain . . . at last . . .

Tuesday, June 11, 1782. The pink glow of dawn was in the sky. Shortly thereafter, the words of George Washington were written:

"It is with the greatest sorrow and concern that I have learned the melancholy tidings of Colonel Crawford's death. He was known to me as an officer of much care and prudence, brave, active and experienced. The manner of his death was shocking . . ."

* * * * * * * *

I began to return to the present, and recalled something that Herman Hesse had written years ago.

Heaps of shards and shambles far and wide.
Thus ends the world.
Thus ends this life of mine.

One never knows what course life will take.

Suddenly Jake's voice broke the stillness. "Recovering artifacts will help with the interpretation of the area and allow us to furnish the buildings more accurately. And at the same time provide material for museum exhibits."

I was numb as he finished talking. My knees felt weak. There was more to history and archeology than I had thought. Not only the material remains of life years ago, but knowledge of the pathos as well. I had already made my decision. There was no turning back now. The die was cast. I would stay.

Getting a marking pencil, I proceeded to write "Hanna's Town" on the bag with the number of my square X - J - 5¼ S.W. (meaning the southwest quarter of the 10-foot square.) Since I was starting with the upper stratum, I wrote 0"-6" for that level. In this way a record of each stratum is kept as accurately as possible, since the correct understanding of a site depends upon the interpretation of the different layers.

Each level can only be dated by the objects found in it. I later learned that if there is any doubt about which layer an artifact came from, it is best to consider it as belonging to the upper one. Less harm is done this way than vice versa, for the level is to be identified by its most recent artifact.

Quickly I wrote down the date and signed my name on the bag. Since I was new at this, the director of archeology very kindly broke the ground for me and took off the grassy turf with a mattock. My job was to open the sods and look for any hidden artifacts before throwing them into the wheelbarrow. Now I was ready to start digging. Jake walked away and left me alone with my task and my thoughts. What meaning did all of this have—the work I was about to begin? Words of Kipling began to form in my mind:

> As a day wears on and the impetus of morning dies away, there will come upon you an overwhelming sense of the uselessness of your toil. This must be striven against.

How do I get myself into situations like this, I wondered. I could be home keeping house. And now all of a sudden I'm out in some farmer's field with a trowel and shovel. And covered with dirt from head to heel. To think that I had tried to get away from dusting! I never knew what dirt really was until now. One never knows what course life will take.

5 • POT LUCK

Once more within the Potter's house alone
I stood surrounded by the Shapes of Clay.

Shapes of all Sorts and Sizes, great and small,
That stood along the floor and by the wall;
And some loquacious Vessels were; and some
Listened perhaps, but never talked at all.

OMAR KHAYYAM

Shortly before arriving at the site I had finished reading a book about archeology and was surprised to learn that excavating one level at a time was not always the way scientists in this field had worked. Prior to the methodical period, archeologists would haphazardly dig with shovels, losing all features, records, and means of dating the artifacts. Then an Englishman by the name of Flinders Petrie came along and started the basic stratigraphy in the late 1800s. He evolved this method of scraping the dirt, layer by layer, and recorded everything found in one stratum before unearthing the next. Petrie realized the importance of "reading" a section from top to bottom in order to establish correctly the sequence of occupation or non-occupation.

I took a five-inch trowel and began once more to scrape and sift the soil, a little at a time—at the level where I had stopped a few days before.

I kept thinking of everything Jake had told me. "If you loosen too much dirt at one time, there is a risk that features may be lost—and once they are destroyed, there is no possible way to make them whole again. A feature is not like a piece of china that can be repaired and put back together."

Later, when you know what to look for, a hoe does the job more quickly than a trowel—but you must always use the trowel in any feature or where there is an abundance of artifacts. And I soon discovered that the side of this tool is used most often. The pointed end is for loosening the soil around an artifact to take it gently out of its place.

I was excited now, for I began to feel that this was my very own square. And it really was mine—at least temporarily. I soon learned that there is an unwritten code among diggers—a sort of squatter's rights. Once you have started a square, that area is yours. No one digs it but you or someone that you designate to help. (The exception is a crash program when a section has to be cleared as soon as possible because the land is needed for other purposes.) And "salting" one another's property with planted artifacts is absolutely taboo.

Speaking of squatters, I soon discovered a handy item to have is a rubber mat. You can either sit or kneel upon it while working with the trowel. It's more for comfort, I have found, than for keeping oneself clean. No matter how careful you are, this is dirty work, literally! And one must not be afraid of getting soiled in the true sense of the word. In fine weather the dirt clings to you enough, but if you get caught in the rain, it is indescribably messy.

As I scraped away with a mason's trowel, a few artifacts came in sight. The first one was a piece of redware. This type of pottery seemed to be prevalent in most sections of the dig, I soon learned through constant discovery. Here on the frontier people lived off the land. They were poor but industrious farmers, and many did not have the wealth that their eastern neighbors had, as shown by their tableware. Most of this earthenware, dating from the Revolutionary War period, was unglazed, but fired very hard in an attempt to make up for lack of non-porous protection. One theory is that there was a scarcity of lead for making glazes at that time.

Research had brought to light the names of some of the potters who had fashioned this ware and were living in the vicinity at the time of Hanna's Town. It was very exciting how tax records revealed their names: Christopher Truby, Jr., Henry Arner, John Cribbs, and Jacob Schloss. I wondered which one of these men had turned this clay on his wheel and later baked it in a kiln. But since the early craftsmen rarely marked their redware with any identification, the mystery would remain unsolved. If only the silent clay could somehow speak, I thought.

At the site, we were fortunate to have our own twentieth-century potter. A young man, attending a nearby Benedictine college, had become interested in Hanna's Town. He began to experiment with the clay taken from our excavations—making earthenware dishes, grease lamps and marbles, reminiscent of what these items would have looked like in years gone by.

"How about scratching your name and the date on the bottoms of all your redware, Mike," someone suggested. "And don't forget to include the words 'Hanna's Town,' too. It sure would make the work a lot easier for future archeologists studying in this area." Unfortunately the redware potters of the past did not have the foresight to do this. They were busy enough just surviving.

The second artifact I found was a piece of distorted, thin green glass. No doubt this was a fragment from an early window. At the time of this discovery I didn't place much importance on a mere sliver of glass from someone's house pane. But later I was told that window glass uncovered at excavations can yield noteworthy information concerning window locations on buildings to be reconstructed.

Just as I was reaching for the trowel, I noticed something white mixed in with the clumps of soil. Picking it up and turning it over in my hand, I examined the shard carefully. On one side it looked similar to the potsherd that Mary Jane had found the first day I had met her. But on the other, I could see the pattern of a design. So this was an example of transfer printing that I had heard fellow excavators speak of from time to time. The engraved drawing had been printed from a copper plate on a thin piece of paper, cut to size, and applied to the ware. When they washed off the paper the pattern adhered to the surface of the clay, which was then ready to be fired in a kiln.

At least by now I could recognize this type of white ware, whether it was plain or decorated. And after finding an abundance of both, I was eager to learn what else I could identify. This new hobby was beginning to get under my skin, as well as under my nails. Now I wanted to have a better knowledge of ceramics. And these criteria really are necessary to tell how early the level is in which you are working. Ceramics are excellent dating tools when it comes to archeology. (Of course another means of dating an area is the carbon 14 method—used best in measuring radioactive carbonized wood or other burnt organic matter. But it is time-consuming, expensive, and for our purposes impractical. Later sites cannot always be measured as accurately as earlier ones.)

Not only does one become interested in dating the ceramics, but also in studying the progress of their development and the changes they have gone through over the years. Many hours can be spent on this typology alone. I realized even more that digging for artifacts not only was time-consuming, but multifaceted as well. It is a more complex undertaking than I had ever guessed.

Not much more than twenty years ago this kind of excavating was scornfully referred to as "tin can archeology" as compared to the ancient digs taking place in Egypt and other eastern countries. It wasn't until recent years that salvage excavating became popular. Now even the scoffers have to admit the importance and value of sifting through every square inch of dirt in order to find the different kinds of ceramics and other artifacts, even something as simple as a straight pin.

Contemplating this, I gathered up the dirt with a short-handled hoe and dust pan. I placed it in the screen and began to sift. I can see why the dirt is screened after it is scraped up, I thought. Many more artifacts show up when the soil is sifted. You think that you see everything when you scrape it, but amazingly enough many important items are missed and only appear in the screening process. The earth is sometimes reluctant to yield what it has carefully guarded for so long.

Continuing with my trowel once more, I noticed another shard coming in sight. It was a smooth, cream-colored one decorated in blue. And it looked very early in origin and old in appearance. I needed help in identifying this one.

In the square next to mine was a friend whom we all knew as Peggy. Having worked at a prehistoric Indian site before coming to Hanna's Town, she was no novice at this kind of thing. Peggy had taken such an interest in the ceramics that—through cleaning them, gluing them back together again, and reading all that she could about the subject—she was fast becoming an expert.

"What luck!" she said. "You found a shard of Bonnin-Morris!"

What I had just discovered, she explained, was an important type of ceramic. Through research, Peggy had learned that this particular porcelain had been made at the Bonnin-Morris factory in Philadelphia sometime between 1770 and 1772. During these years Gausee Bonnin and George Anthony Morris were manufacturing "American China"—a soft-paste, bone-ash porcelain. (The clay came from the banks of the Delaware River near Wilmington and was mixed with calcinated bone.)

"In fact, theirs was the only colonial factory to try to make porcelain on a commercial scale. And this information led to another interesting revelation," she said. "So far, the Bonnin-Morris porcelain factory location in the eastern part of Pennsylvania and the site at Hanna's Town are the only two places where this type of china is recorded as having been found."

Now I appreciated the significance of a simple, plain-looking shard of pottery all the more. And without the basic knowledge of ceramics, one would easily pass it off as an unimportant find.

After Peggy had identified this fragment for me, I came across another one that had blue decor, also. But this one looked different from the others. It was not smooth, but instead had a shiny, pebbly surface and a design scratched into its face.

"This is scratch-blue, a type of white saltglaze stoneware," Peggy said, turning my discovery over in her hand.

And I marveled to myself, "I'll never remember all of that!"

"Now you're really getting into the earlier period," she went on, oblivious to my bewilderment. "Perhaps dating somewhere between 1755 and 1775. As it was being fired, they threw common salt into the kiln and it was absorbed into the atmosphere when the fire was at its hottest. This combined with the silica in the surface of the clay and gave it a slightly pebbled surface. Almost like the skin of an orange," she said. "The design on it was incised and filled with cobalt, a technique borrowed from the Rhineland and popular in the third quarter of the eighteenth century."

I returned to my square much enlightened and enthused now, for not only had I found a rare piece of pottery, but I also had uncovered a type that I had seen at the restored village of Williamsburg, Virginia—where there is an abundance of scratch-blue stoneware which has been discovered in the excavations and even reproduced in great quantities.

Just then my trowel struck something different. What's this? I asked myself. Is it an arrow point? No, it's not made out of flint or any flint-like material. But it surely looks like one, the way the stone is shaped and all, I thought. Perhaps I should save it, just to be sure.

It is commonly known that the Indians made scraping tools and other implements out of stone. Perhaps this was an example of one. As I placed it in my bag, a childhood memory flashed before my eyes. I recalled wading along the banks of Pennsylvania's Wolf Creek with a girl friend one fall day, looking through the shallow ripples as our freezing toes lifted rocks to find the secrets of the stream bed. Looking back I can't remember who found it, but I shall never forget what it looked like. The small flat stone was in the shape of a spear or an arrow point. And carved into the surface on both sides our childish imagination made out an animal footprint, a sword with a jeweled handle, and an eagle with its wings spread in flight.

As true collectors we took our rare find home with us. But the last time I saw my friend she had it and in the meantime was moving to Florida. Where it is now, I shall probably never know. Perhaps it was thrown out upon new soil, hundreds of miles from its origin, only to be discovered again by some starry-eyed youngsters who will once again pick it up and wonder what it was.

By now the wheelbarrow was full. It had filled up sooner than I had expected. I took the screen off and started to push it over to the spoils pile. (All paths lead to this mini-mountain and from every direction, at an archeological dig. It is located at a place that will not get in the way of the work.)

Umph! I couldn't budge the load. I had filled it up too high. Just then Ed, Mary Jane's husband, came over and asked if I would like help with the wheelbarrow. (I'm glad I accepted for this treatment is reserved for beginners only. After you become a veteran, you're strictly on your own, becoming aware of muscles you never knew you had before. And here there is no sex discrimination as far as jobs are concerned. Women have equal opportunity—especially when it comes to hard, physical labor!)

Because of his profession, Ed has taken on the responsibility of archeological draftsman—which every historical site needs. Due to the necessity of many maps of the terrain, he did some investigating into the possibility of borrowing an old drafting table. As a result of his inquiries he was pleasantly surprised when the nuclear research center where he is employed offered it to the historical society at a reduced price. "Seek and ye shall find; ask and it shall be given," he quipped.

In addition to map-making, Ed has done much in the line of surveying, staking out the land, and recording the location of each square on large topographical charts. He and Jake work hand in hand at this. And Ed, being an artist, has drawn in the important features and sketched many pictures for the site for his own pleasure, as well as for publication.

"Thanks, Ed," I said as he returned my wheelbarrow. I made a mental note not to fill it any fuller than what I could handle this time, and I began to scrape the soil once more.

Presently Jake came over to see how I was doing. He scrutinized the profile of my square and then taking a short-handed hoe, he said: "Here, let me show you something. You should never let the sides of your square slope inward as you work. Keep them vertical with right-angled corners, and as neat as possible."

This, I learned, was important, for if the sides are not kept straight the space at the bottom becomes restricted, and if they have to be trimmed later, it becomes almost impossible to decide from which level objects came.

"One of the first signs of an amateur is crooked, sloping walls," Jake went on with a twinkle in his eye.

Well, even though I was a novice, I certainly didn't want to act like one! So I began to make sure the sides were always even from then on.

Pondering as I worked I marveled at how my life had begun to change. Out here like a speck against horizon and sky I had lost myself—drenched in exhilarating work. And in so doing I was beginning to find myself. I was free at last for growth of mind, spirit and soul.

Suddenly the position of the sun reminded me of the time. After working three and a half hours and only going down four inches, I decided that I had had enough for one day. Back at the storage shed I put the wheelbarrow and all my equipment away.

There was a sheet of paper attached to the bulletin board on the wall for everyone to sign in and record the number of hours that he or she worked while at the site each day. So I wrote my signature and jotted down my time. As I proceeded to go over to the spring house to wash my hands and get a drink, Jake met me half way.

"Well, since you're a veteran now, I should tell you where the key is kept in case you come out sometime to dig and no one is here." He led me to the place where the key was and took it off the hook for me to see.

"Just make certain that everything is locked up, if you're the last one to leave," he advised.

I felt as though I had just been handed the key to the city. Surely I had arrived!

6 • PAST TENSE

Earth! you seem to look for something at my hands,
Say, old top-knot, what do you want?

WALT WHITMAN

The day being a Saturday, I took the children and our dachsund with me to Hanna's Town. Brigette, our new puppy, who by a stroke of coincidence was born on my birthday—or was it the other way around—was exuberant, ambling about in a world of her own, with her nose close to the earth in constant search of new and different scents.

This place was not only paradise for a dog, but also for the children, where they could run as deliriously carefree as they pleased. And whenever they would get tired of helping me, which was more times than not, there was always an ample supply of cats and kittens in countless numbers, in addition to the numerous representatives of the canine species that frequented the site—people from time to time taking advantage of the spacious grounds and the good hearts of the caretakers by dropping off unwanted animals.

If this was not enough, there was the ever popular barn to explore with an interesting pond below the hill. Or they would take walks through the fields looking for wild flowers and hiking in the woods with Hanna's Town friends.

As usual the tangle of busy life had obliterated the details of the last trip from my mind and in my square—even though I had covered it with plastic—and the torrential rains had left their mark, too. But after getting the necessary equipment and starting in my section, I remembered that I had already gone down four inches on the stratification of the new square Jake had assigned to me several days earlier. The previous one had not been very fruitful, but this plot was different. I was beginning to find a great number of artifacts. And these chance-treasures are ever under our feet, just waiting to be discovered.

As I worked, I noticed a car drive slowly by and pull off the road into the parking lot. This was not an unfamiliar sight. As the work at Hanna's Town became widely known, more and more people came by to visit it, and there were frequent bus loads of children coming out on excursions during school hours.

On one such occasion our younger son had suggested to his teacher that the history class plan a field trip to the site. This they did and we all had a delightful time eating our lunch on top of the hill overlooking the valley. Even the bus driver, a dear and gentle man with the first name of Tranquil (Honest Injun, it was!) seemed to enjoy the excitement of the day and joined in on the historic tour of the grounds. Usually drivers sit in the bus and doze.

Not only did elementary children come from time to time, but university students as well. One summer a group of twenty workers from the University of Pittsburgh under the direction of their Professor, Dr. James Richardson, helped in the excavation and research to the tune of a six-credit course. And during that time they discovered the former site of a tavern which was known as Foreman's. They uncovered a total of 36 coins—hitting pay dirt in the truest sense of the word—this predominance of money being typical of any tavern grounds. And although these coins had little monetary value to collectors, due to their poor condition after being buried in the ground for many years, they were invaluable to the history of the Hanna's town site.

Now I was down to six inches in my new square when I began to see a stone come in view. As I scraped, it loomed larger and larger. It was covering more territory than it had at first appeared. And it reminded me of something a friend had told me one day in the spring. He said: "A man never knows a piece of ground until he has spaded it." He had just dug a new section of his garden and discovered a huge boulder under the surface. "All those years I have walked over this spot and never knew that monstrosity to be there," he exclaimed.

And now I felt the same as he did. Here was the beginning of another boulder, or so it seemed, as it manifested itself to me. As I continued to go down a layer at a time, the rock not only became wider, but it also was getting thicker. There appeared to be no end to it in sight, and one portion was extending into the next square. But since I was not working on that quarter at the time, I could not unearth it just yet.

This incident reminded me of an archeological case I had recently read about—how a director at an Arabic tell had not let one of the volunteers remove an archaic human skull protruding from his wall for some time until that square was ready to be excavated. And for days while digging he was resigned to working in the presence of the grinning death's head.

If I had been that volunteer, I'm afraid that it would have been too much of a temptation to remove it then and there upon discovery. But you cannot do this at an archeological site, I soon learned. Patience is one of the disciplines that goes along with excavating.

Another discovery was evidence of chinking all around the stone that was uncovered. I took out great amounts of this material which the early settlers used to pack between the logs of their cabins. It was usually made from clay strengthened with wood chips, horse or pig hair, moss, straw, stones, and other binders. And as many an old-timer would say in referring to the need for spring repairs on his abode: "All this house needs is a good daubin."

Just then I found what resembled a small pebble, but since it felt like a lead marble in my hand, I knew immediately that it was a projectile ball from either a smooth-bore musket or a rifle. These bullets were usually made of lead, although pewter was melted down on occasions when other metal was scarce. This particular one still had a mold mark visible on it. Shortly after this I uncovered another which was flattened and spent. Interestingly enough, during the Revolutionary

War soldiers often made "buzzers" or whirligigs for the amusement of the children in military camps from used, flat projectile balls. Archeologists have discovered many of them in British encampment sites in New York and along the Canadian frontier. The teeth at the edges of these leaden discs were placed to the right and left alternately, and with a string they can sound today like eighteenth century humming.

For some reason, it was always exciting to find a musket ball. But one thing that I had not as yet uncovered was a pin—a simple, copper straight pin. The others all around me had discovered them and were even having a pin contest to see who could find the most. And there was I, the simpleton, not having found a single one. I wondered if it was my eyesight or if I wasn't sifting the dirt as carefully as I should. If I could just get one, I'd be satisfied—or so I thought.

All of a sudden my trowel struck a pure-white lucky stone. How on earth did such a smooth pebble ever get here? It must have been brought to this location at one time or another from some distant shore or nearby stream, possibly with road material or sand. This crazy mixed up world, I thought. We did not save these stones for the archeological project, but I did and immediately placed it in my pocket to be used at a later date. For I am a collector—but aren't we all? Besides, another of my interests is painting. Although I mostly paint on large canvases, I enjoy doing miniature pictures on smaller surfaces as well. Perhaps I would paint a picture on it some day. The stone seemed to lend itself to the face of an owl more than anything else. For the time being it would remain among my souvenirs.

Accumulating balls of string and remnants for braided rugs is not exactly my bag. But I am prone to collecting different stones and interesting pebbles. Open any of my purses or pockets and you are likely to find more of these than you do coins. Pity the poor pickpocket or purse thief who is so unfortunate as to pick on me!

But who among us, at some time or another, has never bent over and reached down to the earth for an unusual pebble or a pretty stone that caught the eye? And we turn it over and over in our hand, rubbing off the dirt, and discover one of the finest antiquities of all time—a simple stone. Far older than the earliest civilization of which we have any knowledge, more ancient than humankind itself, dating from a time eons before dinosaurs roamed the earth, or even the first lonely living cell made its initial movement in the primordial ooze.

And as far as collecting goes, remember those trips to the shore? There was always someone who had to bring home a bucket full of curious-looking shells mixed with sand, dried strands of green seaweed, and smelly starfish stashed in the car. But for what purpose? Only to be admired for a brief period and then discarded in the nearest trash can or lost in the family garden.

I have often wondered if in centuries to come our backyard is ever excavated by a group of indulgent archeologists or geologists, what they would think, coming upon myriads of sea shells, fossils, and lucky stones, hundreds of miles inland from places of their origin.

Would they merely say that here once lived a collector who went on numerous vacations to the shore, returning with mementos of the trip, or will they deduce that thousands of years ago these were deposited when the land was deluged by a sea where monsters and great fishes once swam? For all we know, we may be creating future mysteries for those who come after us, when we simply throw out old sea shells and fossils that have lost their interest.

As I was pondering this, one of my twins came over to me. She had gone for a walk down to the spring house and returned with something for me to see. She, too, had made a discovery.

"Look," she said excitedly. "I was just walking along and saw these on the ground." She held out her hand and in it was a piece of glass, beautifully iridescent by long contact with acids in the soil, and a shard of the ubiquitous redware.

"Where did you find them?" I questioned.

"Over there in front of the museum," she said pointing in the general direction.

"That's nice, honey, but don't bring me any more. If you see other broken glass or dishes lying on the ground, leave them there. But since you've already found these, put them in the shed on the shelf that is marked 'surface finds.'" (Sometimes this instant seizure becomes a necessity, however, for in places the artifacts are prominently in view, and in order to protect them from getting broken or taken by passersby, it is a good idea to salvage the items immediately. A surface find such as a coin or anything else of obvious value should always be rescued upon discovery, and marked as to where it was found.)

As she disappeared to do what she was told I mused over the situation. This is another way that artifacts get misplaced and in the wrong layer, chronologically. For if I were to put these surface finds in my bag now, which is at the 6"-12" level, it would only create confusion.

Shortly, a group of people came to visit the site. After observing us at work for some time, one small boy piped up eagerly: "If you find some old thing ya' don't want, I'll take it."

Amused by this remark, Joan, another volunteer—replied: "This is one place where the older the thing is, the more valuable it becomes and the more we want it. But if we find something nice and new, we'll be sure to save it for you."

And I thought, how true this has become. For not only are archeologists preoccupied with the old in preference to the new, but people in all occupations have become interested in scrounging around for some old dirty, dust-laden object rather than in buying something modern or a reproduction in the clean, orderly surroundings of a conventional store.

But even dealers in antiquities are waking up to the fact that people aren't always interested in discovering antiques that are clean and sorted in a systemic fashion. They want a little adventure, as well. The buyers many times prefer to search through old, hay-strewn barns looking for something unusual and with the pervasive dust of time still clinging to it. In this case, in contrast to house-cleaning, to dust merely takes away some of the value and romance, in the eyes of the purchaser.

And as we look back we can remember all the old things that we threw out years ago in the name of junk, and now kick ourselves every time we come across the very same things in antique stores across the country. And with fancy prices on them, to boot!

I recall overhearing a conversation at a flea market recently. A shocked woman had pulled one of her friends aside and whispered. "Tell me, Mabel, am I seeing things, or is that penny candy jar, in the shape of a boat—like the one that my son had been playing store with—really marked $15.00." And along the same vein of thought, a nearby sign read: "We buy junk and sell treasures." Unfortunately, most of us do not have enough foresight to recognize our commonplace items of everyday use as being valuable merchandise of the future.

Perhaps this trend toward an interest in the past is a sign of the times. Although there is much to be said on behalf of industry in the ways of luxury, convenience, and a more carefree life—and I would be among the last to want to give it up, for if it weren't for my washer and dryer at home, I wouldn't have time to dig!—it still has backfired in more ways than pollution alone. Our mass productive way of life is not conducive to the quality and longevity in its wares to match those of the earlier craftsmen. For one thing, it almost seems as though industry does not want products to last that long anyway—built-in obsolescence for more buying power. But, of course, in all fairness to industry, it is governed by what consumer demand will tolerate.

Or it may be that the intense new intrigue in the former way of life reflects the insecurity of our future, dissatisfaction with the present, and a desire to turn to the warmth of what we imagine was in the past. (Sometimes, when we wish to return to those days, we forget about the drafty log houses and the lack of modern conveniences—which only proves that every generation in time has its own unique problems.)

This longing to revert to the simple homespun ways of our forefathers has come about due to the fast, frantic pace of the complex, neon-sign and glitter world that engulfs us in artificiality. In spite of the carefree plastic items that are on the market today, many people still prefer the warmth of wood. The culture in which we are living is so much influenced by the razzle-dazzle of commercialism that dull wood tones become a welcome relief.

Our ancestors experienced the opposite. Theirs was a much plainer and more drab life-style. Most of their household items were made of wood. To them it was commonplace. We cherish wood, for it is becoming scarcer and more expensive. (Hang on to your empty wooden thread spools, for they will soon be collectables, too.)

A fine example of this yearning for brighter surroundings in a plain culture is seen in the Pennsylvania Germans, more commonly but erroneously referred to as the Pennsylvania Dutch. In order to achieve contrast, they painted their drab furniture with bright, gay colors and elaborate decor. Just as they covered up the monotonous wood grains, we many times remove the colorful paint from old furniture and restore it to the natural wood tones—much of which is scratched and worn by generations of use.

And so with the changing of times, more and more people are finding a new love in antiques, bottle hunting, and in digging up what is gone but only half forgotten. Many want to revive certain aspects of bygone days. There is charm ir objects which have spanned the centuries.

In this attempt to recapture the past, we find ourselves reproducing even the defects of bygone days. The early craftsmen apologized for the rough-hewn logs with ax or adze marks visible on their surfaces, for they wanted them to be as sooth and perfect as possible. But today we manufacture ceiling beams intentionally producing imperfections and rustic textures, regardless of the availability of modern tools and machinery to make flawless ones. We do this because the world has become too commercialized. Collecting and living with antiques and their environment is like an escape from our modern day intrusions. But the idea is not to live in the past, but to hold on to it.

As I was thinking this over, the lad was rewarded. For he became interested through his own curiousity that he asked if he could help screen—which we gladly let him do, and he found new things along with the old.

This, then is a job where there is no discrimination against age. In fact amateur (or citizen) archeologists of all ages play an important role since there are not enough professionals to carry out the work that needs to be done at countless historic sites across America. And archeology is one of the few scientific fields that still give nonprofessionals a chance to contribute. School boys and girls can offer much to a historical site and may even become regular recruits in time.

Such is the case with Pete, who lived in the "mine patch Hannastown" about a mile down the road from the site. Pete and I came to the dig about the same time. He was still in high school and very much interested in archeology and local history. At first Pete was shy, and hardly ever said a word. But he was a good and faithful worker. Always at the site, willing and ready with a helping hand, he was learning and in time found his tongue. The first day that I met him, I would never have guessed that some day he would be speaking about Hanna's Town before groups of students and adults alike. But this wasn't all. After uncovering a great number of buckles and buttons, Pete decided to conduct a study of them. The types were diversified—brass, silver, pewter, and bone. Pete had discovered a silver buckle with the initials S.F. engraved on it—who knows, maybe it belonged to Sarah Foreman, the tavern owner's wife. How helpful it is to researchers in trying to unravel the mysterious shadows of the past, when people engrave their initials on personal possessions!

Pete had also discovered a button die in the fort area, and a button made from this mold was uncovered across the road from it a short time later. The county historical society had reproductions of this button made from pewter as special mementos of the dig, and also for sale as a money-making project so that our endeavors can continue.

Just recently a youth program for students interested in learning the procedures of archeological digging was begun at the site. And I can't help thinking what an excellent opportunity this is for active "young" people of all ages. The only necessary requirements are a sincere interest, a love of the out-of-doors, and a willingness to work.

One becomes so entrenched (no pun intended) in this sort of activity, that there is no time nor need for drugs or tranquilizers. The earth itself is both an intoxicating stimulant of interest and a pacifier that can either keep one high or provide a spirit of serenity. Anyone who has gotten back to the earth, thoroughly engulfed in whatever he or she enjoys doing the most, knows that this is true.

It is the balance of life that is refreshing. By escaping through our creative outlets and renewing our inner springs, we can come back to our daily work and routine with enthusiasm. And likewise, fatigued by practical jobs, we welcome a change through outside interests.

While I pondered this, I was reminded of a visitor who stopped at the site one day. During his conversation with a friend and me, he related to us his own interest in archeology and the various Indian artifacts he had found over the years. Then he leaned over, and in a low voice as if he were going to tell a secret, he revealed how all his life he had been close to nature, learning much from it. And so convinced by its therapeutic qualities, he said: "It is good for a person to work with his hands in the earth—for it has healing powers." What he said reminded me of a bit of doggerel by John K. Bangs:

> To dig and delve in nice clean dirt,
> Can do a mortal little hurt.

I looked at my dirty hands and laughed at the time and suddenly I felt very healthy. Now, in retrospect, I wonder if there really wasn't something to what he had said. The earth does indeed furnish all our needs, if we could only recognize them, putting natural resources to the most beneficial use—not destructively, but for the good of its people.

With the ever increasing interest in ecology there has been a growing concern over our environmental problems. People are beginning to return to the earth, reawakened to the land as the aborigines knew it centuries ago. They were keenly aware of the importance of conserving native resources and were conscious of the value of natural foods not only for healthful purposes but for treating human ailments. Today herbal societies are springing up as a result of this revival of interest in humankind's welfare and survival. And people are exchanging knowledge as well as plants.

As I was preparing to leave that same day, another group

came to visit. They had just emerged from the springhouse museum.

"What a peaceful spot," a woman among them said as her eyes came to rest on the garland of trees and tombstones encircling the hilltop which overlooks the site.

"Yes," I agreed. "It is now. But it wasn't always so. That peak you see is known as "Gallows Hill" and it was the scene of several hangings shortly after the Revolutionary War—in fact, the first recorded act of capital punishment west of the Alleghenies. An Indian was to be hanged for murdering a white man (after getting drunk on white man's whiskey). But just before his death he heard that a young girl was suffering from an illness. He asked that he might be set free so that he could go into the woods to procure a certain herb that would make her well again. The men released him and the Indian returned with the plant which saved the life of the child—but unfortunately not his own.

"And when Hanna's Town was attacked and burned, that same hill no doubt was active and alive with the sound of battle as Indians and British soldiers swarmed over it."

The woman and I were looking in that direction when all of a sudden we were startled by the sound of horses' hooves coming from the other side. The peace and tranquility of the scene was sharply interrupted by the trumpet blast of a horn. Over the summit dashed a dozen or more horsemen from a nearby hunt club—wearing red and black riding outfits, creating a most spectacular scene. The Redcoats were surely coming again!

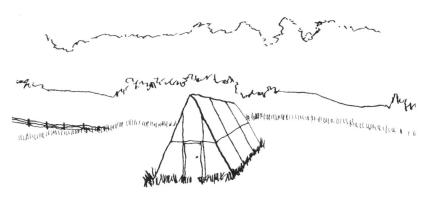

7 • ALL WORK AND NO PLAY

Undaunted by December,
The sap's faithful yet.
The giving earth remembers,
And only men forget.
  JOHN G. NEIHARDT

Hanna's Town became more interesting day by day. But these days shortened and magically another season had arrived.

Although summer was the peak of physical work at the site, the onset of winter did not mean an end to activity. It was during these months that the volunteers, with more time on their hands, could do research—looking up old land deeds, wills, accounts, and documents; probing diligently into genealogical records, journals, diaries, and archives for information that would shed some light on a particular discovery; or searching for early maps that would help with the location of streets, property, and other topographical knowledge.

Volunteers such as Jean, Arlene, Cathy, and Ann were literally working night and day on this. Old church records and tax lists provided them with a constant source of information—and often frustration as well.

But the rewards are worth it. For instance, just recently they uncovered an account of an early pastor in Hanna's Town in 1773. Searching through the old Donegal

Presbytery records on microfilm (since the old Redstone Presbytery was not yet in existence here in what was then wilderness) Jean came across a Rev. Mr. Huey who was referred to as a "slippery character." In the settlers' words, "He lifted the bowl to his face too often." Not only was he known as a habitual imbiber, but he also committed an unforgivable sin of that era. It so happened that he had lost his silk Barcelona handkerchief and had therefore decided to persuade the storekeeper in Hanna's Town to sell him one on the Sabbath. (A parson breaking Pennsylvania's Sunday blue law!) This seemed to be a good enough excuse to oust him from the ministry. By the way, the helpful storekeeper was also reprimanded for having sold it to him in the first place.

But the most significant thing to us was the fact that in relating this event and the ensuing trial the writer of that day gave a good description of the interior of Hanna's courthouse-tavern and also the certainty that there really was a store in Hanna's Town. Previous historians and articles had led us to believe that there was no such thing as a true shop, other than those in the taverns, in the county-town. So thanks to Mr. Huey we gained valuable information for the site. Research never ceases to bring discoveries and enlightenment!

So far no one has found a map showing the layout of the original town. Perhaps this, too, will turn up some day, tucked away in someone's attic among long forgotten papers. In recent years Dr. Jane Clotworthy, a thoughtful woman, donated an old horsehair trunk with letters from her family—letters which had been passed on from one generation to another, with the wax seals still clinging to them (no envelopes in those days)—and dating back to the eighteenth century, dropping such names as George Washington and Arthur St. Clair. One never knows in the field of research where or when something of value will appear.

Winter, too, was the time when most of the artifacts were cleaned, sorted, and numbered. And since I usually let mine accumulate during the summer months without washing and counting them each day—as many of the others did—I really had my work cut out for me.

We now not only had our own field museum at the site, but

our artifacts were also on display at the Westmoreland Historical Society in the art museum of Greensburg. Things were progressing.

In addition to behind-the-scenes work going on at this time, there was still some digging, in spite of inclement weather. Several of the volunteers had gotten together to build an A-frame structure enclosed in plastic to be moved on top of any square that was to be dug. This not only kept the ground from being covered with snow, but protected the excavators from the wind and rain as well. And there was even a heater inside for warmth. (Brigette happened to get caught beneath the frame once as it was being moved from one place to another and she almost became wienerwurst for sure!)

During a turbulent storm one night, a great gust of wind lifted the A-frame high into the air like Dorothy's house in *The Wizard of Oz*. It came down with a crash, and the plastic covering shattered into many pieces. To this day anyone who happens to dig in the area where it landed is continually frustrated by finding bits and fragments of the original reinforced polyester, mistaking it at times for shards of china. I know—I was one of those fooled.

On another occasion I was deceived by what I thought was a rare type of pottery. It was rough on one side, smooth on two, and rounded on the fourth—quite different and impressive looking. I showed my unusual discovery to Pete and he laughed with a guffaw.

"Oh, you found some 'wheelbarrows.'"

"And what, may I ask, is that?" I said.

"Well, mud sometimes gets lodged in the metal underparts of the wheelbarrow. When it dries and falls out, you end up with a clay cast of the hollowed areas of the frame."

That took the wind out of my sails!

This incident reminded me of my first day at the site. I had found snake-like clay fragments which I thought were some ancient specimens of stoneware. They turned out to be hardened mud tread marks left in the ground by twentieth-century truck tires—another case of mistaken identity.

But it isn't all work at Hanna's Town, especially in the off-season months. There are many fringe benefits as well. Although I had found a new interest, an artist can never lay aside the paint brush for long. In fact there seldom was a time in my life that I was not painting or drawing—with whatever was available or convenient at the moment, even with house paint if necessary.

And here at Hanna's Town was a paradise to put onto a canvas. It is too much of a temptation to pass up. It would be impossible for any aesthete not to be filled to overflowing with a desire to reproduce the harmonious landscape, the endless rolling hills, the splendor of the view from on top of Gallows Hill, and the continuous seasonal changes which are particularly outstanding along the countryside. When you live close to nature, you cannot be insensitive to its grandeur—its eternal beauty.

Our children, of course, became my finest critics. Their clarity of vision is unbiased. Looking over my shoulder they will tell me with honest-to-goodness truth exactly what is wrong with my sketches. It is not always flattering, but extremely helpful.

Here, too, I had reacquainted myself with nature. One day while walking through a field near the site I almost stumbled over a newly born fawn asleep in the tall grass. It didn't seem to be the least disturbed upon opening its large, pensive brown eyes and looking up at the strange creature staring down at it in wonder.

To have my own eyes opened again to nature has been a most delightful experience. Somehow in the process of raising a family I had lost sight of the mighty out-of-doors. But for one who is a naturalist at heart, it did not take much to become reawakened to it once again. A closeness to nature helps bring more understanding to life.

For one thing, I was always interested in plants, and Hanna's Town with its open fields and endless verdure, along with its woods and streams, supplied me with a great source for my new and renewed interests.

It was at this time that I had an opportunity to meet the late Euell Gibbons, the naturalist and writer who was sometimes referred to as the wild man of Central Pennsylvania—not on account of his habits but because of his knowledge and use of the flora and fauna in this part of the country. (Did you ever eat a pine tree?)

After attending one of his interesting seminars in Landis Valley at the Institute of Pennsylvania Rural Life and Culture, I came home with the inspiration to learn all that I could about our native edible wild plants, too—the process of making maple syrup from the sap of trees, how daylily buds can be as delicious as fresh green beans, and even how you can make flour from acorns and cattail roots.

With utmost care I foraged plants from each season— freezing, drying, and preserving them, many times reminiscent of the way foods had to be preserved and stored back in the days of Hanna's Town. (Extreme care must be given in such an undertaking, however, for some poisonous plants can be mistaken for the nonpoisonous ones. And this could be disastrous.)

The following spring brought forth another abundance of greenery, and we decided that it was a good time to have our own "wild party" such as Euell Gibbons was accustomed to preparing, and use nothing but the plants that I had gleaned from Hanna's Town and other places nearby, along with the fresh ones that could be picked in this season that was upon us.

(About the only food not garnered from the site was the lake trout that my husband and I had caught while on a fishing trip with my father and the children in Canada. But we still considered it wild—especially after recalling the frenzied time that we had in getting those fish into the boat! And the mushrooms—we just did not trust ourselves in identifying them. So instead we bought fresh ones from a supermarket and jokingly told our guests not to worry—we had the children pick them for us.)

In preparing the food I was thrilled to discover for the first time, what was common knowledge to most people, but was new to me—the wonder of jelly. Natural pectin in the crabapples made it all jell in such mysterious beauty before my very eyes.

At first I didn't think that we would have enough variety in the menu to be interesting. But at the end of the year when we took stock of what had been preserved, there was enough for two parties. (By the way, with the high cost of living, the record-breaking price of beef, and lettuce being so exorbitant at times, this is a unique way to entertain—much preparation but at a minimal expense—and usually a once in a life-time experience because of the work and time involved. But it is a menu that guests will remember for a long time.) My friend, Charmaine, wrote all about the wild dishes in her cook's corner of the local newspaper: Jerusalem artichokes, dandelion wine, mint and violet salad (using both leaves and flowers of the violet plant—which, by the way, is just as pretty as it is good, having more vitamin C than lettuce—) milkweed buds which taste as good as broccoli, daylily soup, wild blackberry pie, crabapple jelly, sassafras tea, and poke, a weed whose berries are poisonous, but not the leaves. (The tender new shoots are, according to some, better than asparagus.) And it's all a free gift from nature.

Wayside verdure at Hanna's Town has not only supplied us with a unique way of entertaining, in addition to the endless variety of foods, but it has helped me in the teaching of my craft classes as well. The ever versatile corn plant provides material for many ideas. For example, corn husk dolls—that today are for the most part imported from other countries and are seen on shelves of gift shops across the nation—were originally our own native craft. It was taught to the early settlers by the Indians—maize being first introduced to white men by these natives.

From this wonderful plant we not only obtain a delicious food, but also husks which can be lightened in the sun or soaked in a laundry bleach to make them clean. Used as they are, following this treatment, or tinted—either with commercial dyes or natural ones such as berries for red shades and walnut hulls for brown—they make beautiful flowers, wreaths, and table centerpieces. Every single part of this plant has a use.

The fields around Hanna's Town awakened me creatively to our native flora, and as a result I have even made new friends when asking the owners' permission to forage natural materials from their fields for my craft classes. I have discovered interests above ground as well as below its surface.

Hanna's Town has provided enjoyment for others as well. The top of Gallows Hill is an excellent spot for watching spectacular fireworks, for which the neighborhood of Crabtree is famous in the month of July. And in the late summer, the Historical Society has its annual corn roast and meeting on the restoration grounds.

Of course, to us volunteers, it is a convenient place for getting together after work for family cookouts in which most of the conversation centers around the dig and the latest discoveries that we all are eager to share with one another. Through such stimulating discussions as these, I am even more aware of the literal interpretation of the word archeology, which is derived from the Greek words, *Archaeos*—meaning of the past, and *logos*—signifying discourse.

And although archeology, in the physical sense, is essentially digging and excavating, the work is seldom boring. There is continuous suspense associated with it that accompanies every dig. It may sound as dry as the dust it involves, but so far there has never been a dull moment for me. And the adventure is not only in the earth; it encompasses the surroundings of the historic site as well.

Take the time that the Appalachian wagon train came to Hanna's Town. This was an event which people came from miles around to see. The members of this organization—inspired by a group of people, who in 1963 traveled in covered wagons from North Wilkesboro to Boone, North Carolina, following the trail Daniel Boone led early settlers over years ago—decided to form their own wagon train. And it proved to be so successful, that it has come to be an annual event.

But our county's bicentennial celebration in 1973 marked the greatest number of participants they had ever had. And anyone owning a covered wagon could join—a rather exclusive qualification to be sure!

That year more than seventy wagons traveled for fifty miles on their trek from Somerset to Hanna's Town. Dressed in clothing reminiscent of the pioneers, the families—to some degree—re-enacted what the hardy early settlers must have endured in conquering the wilderness as they pushed westward over the mountains. The trip was repeated for the nation's bicentennial three years later.

I will long remember the thrilling sight of men, women, children, and even family pets riding in covered wagons—some authentic Conestogas and others improvised—making their way down the highway and into the grounds at Hanna's Town. Along with the horses was a team of beautiful red oxen—these beasts truly representative of how many of the pioneers traveled in those early days. As the train entered the site, the wagons made a large circle and camped there for the night. After supper, when evening was drawing to a close, the wagoners and their families gathered around the camp fire, singing songs from bygone days. The next morning, after breakfast, they had a church service within the enclosure of wagons with the sky overhead as their cathedral. How exciting it must have been for these people, to relive some of the experiences of the past and to appreciate more fully the hardships our forefathers had to endure.

In even more recent years Civil War-time re-enactments are carried out at Hanna's Town with candlelight tours through improvised Union and Confederate army camps.

It was not only the enthusiasm and the warm-hearted people that day, but the continuous parade of visitors each and every day at the site that has made the dig worthwhile. Almost every hobby and sport is dependent in some respect upon its spectators and a constant supply of "sidewalk superintendents" as well as its participants, to make it a fulfilling endeavor. We are working to restore the town for others as well as ourselves.

How could anyone become bored with such a hobby, I asked myself! A past time has brought me back to the earth and has enriched my life with its endless wonder. I have never felt so much alive!

CORN HUSK BROOM

1. Use tree branch (remove bark) for handle. 2.   Place bleached, damp, field-corn husks around bottom of handle. Tie securely. Trim uneven ends. 3.   Fold down top edges of husks. Tie in place with cord or a corn husk. 4.   Shred loose bottom husks with a large needle. Trim.

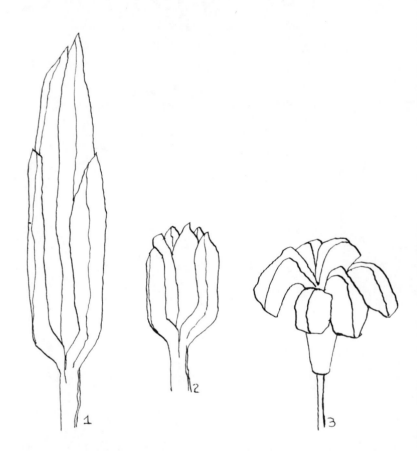

CORN HUSK FLOWERS
1.   Bleach corn husks while still attached to stalk, using one part bleach to four parts water. Dye with commercial or natural colors (optional). 2.   Cut corn husks while still damp, in shape of petals, about three inches from stalk. 3.   Roll each petal separately on a pencil or wooden-spoon handle. For arranging in a vase, tape dried teasel stems to stalks.

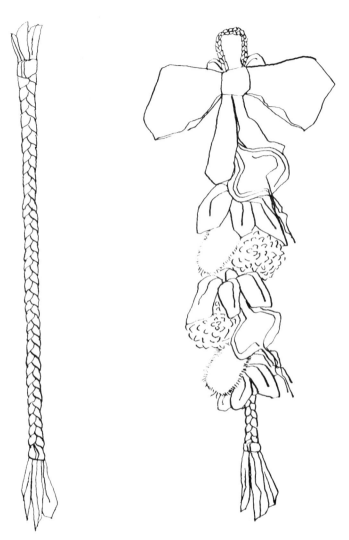

CORN HUSK KITCHEN SWAG

1. Braid bleached, damp corn husks together until about 20" long. When husks become too short add more husks to the braid. 2. Wire corn-husk flowers, garlic bulbs, straw flowers, or teasel to braid. 3. Attach corn-husk bow or ribbon bow to top of swag. Add a small, braided corn-husk loop for hanging.

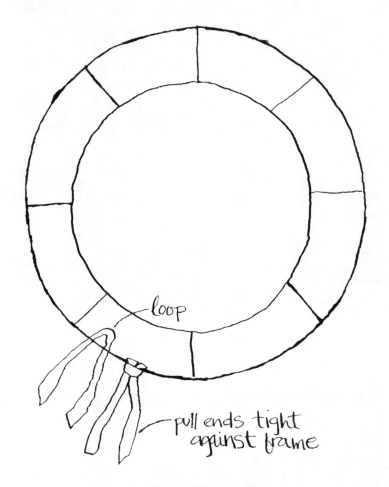

CORN HUSK WREATH

1. Start with a wire-wreath frame (can be purchased at a craft or floral shop). 2. Attach bleached damp corn husks, about an inch in width but using their natural length, to frame according to illustration above. 3. Fold husk ends back and draw through loop (around frame). Pull tight and add next husk. Repeat until wreath is finished. 4. When frame is completely covered (with no wire showing), shred husks with large needle. If material dries before completion, redampen. After the husks have all been shredded, they will start to curl as they dry. 5. Add a bow to the finished wreath (optional). 6. Wreath may be washed in mild detergent and water.

MILKWEED CHEDDAR CHEESE CASSEROLE

Cook eight cups of tender, new milkweed buds (before pink blossoms form), and small leaves in water. Boil for three minutes. Change water and repeat process two more times (to get rid of bitterness).

Place cooked vegetables in greased casserole and pour cheese sauce over contents. Bake 15-20 minutes. Serves about 8.

Cheese Sauce

1 tbsp. butter
1 tbsp. flour
¼ tsp. salt
¼ tsp. dry mustard
¼ tsp. onion salt
1/8 tsp. pepper
1 cup milk
½ cup Cheddar cheese, cubed or shredded

Directions: Melt butter over low heat in heavy saucepan. Blend in flour, seasonings. Add cheese and milk, stirring constantly until smooth and thick. Boil one minute.

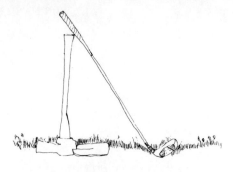

8 • LIFTING THE TURF

Perhaps it is because he hears a different drummer.
Let him step to the music he hears, however measured or far away.
HENRY DAVID THOREAU

"All right—who took my mattock?" demanded Jim.

"No one shiftless enough to be a thief would want to steal one of those back-breaking tools," answered Charlie.

Charlie had more than a casual interest in Hanna's Town. He, his wife, and seven children live in a historic stone house, partly constructed of logs. Charlie had become curious about this home when it was deserted—a shambles with broken windows and only half a roof. But with the eye of an artist and an interest in history he saw the potential. There was a heritage here to be saved. He talked it over with his family, and they decided to buy it.

At the time, Charlie and Aline were living in a new, modern house; and all their friends and relatives thought that they had either lost their fortune or their minds. But with much determination and hard work, they restored the old ruin to a beautiful and outstanding home. The date 1776 was carved on the door under many layers of various colored paints, and in the process of restoration they discovered a note belonging to an indentured servant, hidden in a secret compartment behind a stone in the dining room wall.

But perhaps the most significant thing of all was the fact that the White brothers—the original builders and owners of this house—upon hearing of the burning of Hanna's Town in the year 1782, rode their horses with others back and forth across a foot bridge near the fort in the middle of the night during the attack. The scheme to deceive the Indians worked, and the savages left before dawn thinking that there were many reinforcements coming to aid the settlers trapped within the fort. So there was a direct connection between the house that Charlie and his family lived in and the historic site where he came to dig.

Working in the square next to Charlie were Helen and Kirke. This kind of thing was not new to them, for they had dug on Indian sites before coming to Hanna's Town. And their house held many interesting artifacts—room after room filled with bags of them. When they said that there was a skeleton in their closet, they meant it!

Helen was familiar with the process of identifying different types of ceramics; and before long she and Peggy were working as a team, cataloguing and cementing pieces back together again. They both stored myriads of potsherds that had been cleaned and were waiting to be made as nearly whole again as possible by these two industrious women.

Presently Kirke strolled over to where I was digging and lit a cigarette. I showed him what I had found so far. Looking into the bag he saw bits of metal, bone, a large musket ball and many shards of redware.

"Well, I see you found quite a prolific square for yourself," he commented. As we talked back and forth, Kirke told me the latest news about the rattlesnake flag with the motto, "Don't Tread On Me." Three of the volunteers—the Caesar family—were planning to reproduce this famous banner that Colonel John Proctor, the first sheriff at Hanna's Town, had used for his battalion during the Revolutionary War.

"As you know from history, this flag had a snake with thirteen rattles on it representing the colonies that were in rebellion against England," he went on. "In the center of the field the rattler is coiled, with the head erect, in the attitude of striking the British Union Jack in the upper right-hand corner. A symbolic threat to Great Britain if she didn't shape up."

After chatting for some time, Kirke remarked: "Well—I had better get that mattock to working again. It's not 'auto-mattock,' you know." Kirke was always a great kidder. You couldn't take yourself seriously around him. He helped make the excavating more like fun than anything else, and his Scotch-Irish humor was a delight to everyone.

As I resumed my own work, I suddenly unearthed a thin green object that looked very much like a blade of grass. I yelled and Kirke turned to see what all the excitement was about.

"I found a pin!" I exclaimed, practically jumping up and down. "A straight pin."

But Kirke, having uncovered many of these tin-coated copper alloy pins by this time, did not seem to share my enthusiasm over the discovery. "I'll get you a container to keep it in," he offered placidly. "If you put that in your bag along with everything else—dirt included—you'll never see it again."

Walking over in the direction of the shed, he soon returned with an empty film cartridge. Anything special, small, or fragile is placed in containers such as these for safe keeping before being put into the bag with the rest of the artifacts.

After the first one, I began to find many more straight pins—and some not so straight—in this square. Evidently I had never excavated where there were pins, until now. Possibly my eyesight wasn't as poor as I was beginning to think. Or was it the experience of digging that made me more observant than I had been in the beginning? This I would never know—but at least I had made my discovery. And I began to find enough to compete in the contest along with the others.

This sudden observation is typical of humans, for some reason. Once we discover something that is new to us in life, we are likely to continue finding more. We are instantaneously impressed with an awareness of what was around us all the time, but to which we were oblivious, before.

To be more explicit, just recently a new plant manifested itself to me. The children discovered it growing along the side of the road. It resembled a dandelion that had gone to seed, but the flower portion was four times as large with a stem three feet long.

Later a friend told me that this plant was called goat's

beard. Shortly thereafter, while enroute on our vacation, I related this revelation to my husband and all of a sudden, quite as if by magic, we saw a whole field of them growing along the highway. After that occasion, we began to see these plants other places as well.

My friend said that she had a similar experience with latent recognition. As a child, she had tried to understand the principles of shadow and line in art class, yet without much success. And then, one day while lying under a tree—just as Sir Isaac Newton had—she gazed up into its spreading branches and suddenly saw line and shadow for the very first time. After this enlightenment, she was conscious of her newly discovered phenomena in everything that she observed.

So it was with the pins. Now they were everywhere. Then I thought in a chiding manner, how could anyone be so happy over finding pins that someone had lost years ago? I lose these items around the house all the time. But here was I, overjoyed at the very sight of one old, corroded, straight pin! Was I losing my mind along with the pins? Or was this a typical reaction of anyone engrossed in archeology?

After the novelty of discovering a pin—along with others like it—had worn off I thought, now if only I can find an old coin. But isn't this just like human nature for you? We work diligently to get something, and then when that which we have struggled for is at last attained, we are no longer satisfied and want something else. We are never content. But perhaps this is the essence of progress. If we were resigned to the bare necessities of life, there would be no incentive for growth or improvement. In the words of the Lebanese prophet, Kahlil Gibran: "For man is happy only in his aspirations to the heights. When he attains his goal, he cools and longs for other distant flights."

So I found myself wishing for a coin from the Hanna's Town period. That would be great, I thought.

My hopeful thinking reminded me of my father's philosophy in life. "Never wish for lost money, for your gain would only be someone else's loss." And with this reflection of wisdom in mind, I rationalized to myself: In this situation I would not be wishing for money lost in our time. A coin dropped by a person who had lived two hundred years ago was certainly different. Their loss was no longer felt. And besides, to retrieve a coin from the past for the museum display would please not only myself, but others as well. So I went on with my wishful thinking.

As I dug down through the layers I soon realized that I had come to a midden—what every archeologist wants to discover. The dirt was darker and softer here, and I could tell by the enormous number of artifacts coming out of it that this spot had once been someone's rubbish pit. In places the ground was red where it had been burned and black pieces of charcoal were beginning to show up in the soil.

All of a sudden my eyes spied something unusual. I picked it up and discovered that it was a brass ring—perhaps someone's lost wedding band. I pondered how it had gotten here in the first place. Was the owner of this treasured piece of jewelry burning her trash at the time of its loss, or was it thrown out accidentally?

I recalled that according to tradition there had been a wedding the day that Hanna's Town was attacked by the Indians. It took place at Miller's blockhouse a short distance away from the village. And many of the Hanna's Town residents were there for the occasion.

I wonder what it would have been like to be married in those days—starting out by having to construct your own house from scratch with hand tools? (Today when we speak of building our homes, we really mean that an architect, contractor, and group of carpenters, plumbers, masons, and electricians actually did the task and we paid the bill.) And having to set up housekeeping with only the very barest of necessities must have been difficult. I do not imagine that they were very concerned over dusting and polishing furniture in those days on the frontier. Worse yet, there was the constant worry of being attacked by Indians each day of existence. For these people, that fear became a reality. The wedding party's infare never occurred, and they were forced to march as captives to Canada.

I looked at the ring once more before placing it in a special container. It had suddenly taken on more meaning. I could imagine the great disappointment and the search that must have gone on to recover it. All in vain! And now, many years later, it shows up. But the story behind it and the identity of the wearer are gone forever. It is ironic, for whoever she was had had the knowledge that I wanted—but not the ring. And I now possessed the treasure—but knew nothing about it. The mystery would remain unsolved to the end of time. *C'est la vie!*

This find was soon followed by a thimble, bits of chinking, pieces of bricks, rusted square nails, more musket balls, sundry ceramics, and a man's stick pin for a cravat—as they called ties in earlier days. Here had truly been someone's favorite trash spot.

Perhaps, I conjectured, it had been moving day for these people. And they had gotten rid of their old junk, burning it down to the ashes.

How many times we, too, have had to sort our earthly possessions in order to move them from one household to the next—only to stand there scratching our chins in bewilderment. Where did it all come from? How in the world did we ever accumulate all this junk in the first place?

Frank Lloyd Wright once wrote "There is no reason for people to hold on to so much junk," and furthermore he did not believe in cellars or attics for this reason. In general, though, we mortals are such pack rats! And we proceed to sort it all out and get rid of it. Even the most meticulous housekeeper becomes aware of this dilemma at some time or another. And at last when our homes are once more clean and orderly, we are ready to start all over again—saving and hoarding odds without ends.

But the age-old earth still clings to much of what we thought was gone forever. It has often been said, "What is one man's trash is another one's treasure." In years to come someone may be delighted with potsherds that we have left behind and take great pleasure in trying to piece together the meaning of broken dishes and fragments of jewelry that we have discarded.

Since I was well into a pit area now and was finding many new kinds of ceramics along with the other artifacts, it was time that I at least learned the evolution of the eighteenth-century pottery without always having to bother my fellow workers. So I did some homework.

Excluding coarse earthenwares, slipwares, and stonewares, the sequence is as follows: delftware to white saltglaze, saltglaze to creamware, and creamware to pearlware, in that order. It wasn't until the nineteenth century that ironstone became popular.

Now at least I could put the ceramics in some kind of chronological order in my mind. I knew that delft was thick, with a soft, orange paste inside, usually with a dull blue and white design. It had lost its popularity around 1730 due to its easy breakage and was replaced by a more durable ware.

Creamware, later called Queen's ware—so named when Queen Charlotte of England started to use it—was the cornerstone of Josiah Wedgewood's prosperity in the 1750s and on into the 1770s. A greenish-yellow cast is most readily noticed on creamware at the junctions of handles and areas where the glaze accumulated thickly in the process of manufacture. Pearlware, developed by Wedgewood in 1779, has more of a bluish tint—that can be seen best in the same corresponding places as creamware. Of course, I already knew what saltglaze and ironstone looked like.

All of a sudden I saw something that was definitely not ceramic. There was no mistaking what it was. I had found a coin! And not a new one, but a very early one. I could hardly wait to touch it. After picking it up I gently rubbed the surface dirt off. My exclamations created a quick audience and everyone gathered around me to see what I had found. This time they were excited, too. There was a date on the coin and it was still legible. But before I had a chance to decipher what it was, John said, "Here, let me see it," taking my new discovery from me for further examination. What a find, I thought. Not only pins and a ring, but a coin as well. This was indeed my lucky day.

"You certainly found an early one," Gretchen rejoiced, "1776?"

"It looks like it's Spanish," remarked Don.

"Two reale, to be exact," added Kirke.

Kirke handed the treasure to Jake. "Let's see . . . that was worth about two bits in English money," he said.

(Two bits, four bits, six bits, eight bits make a dollar, I counted to myself. It must be a Spanish quarter.)

"But of course the date on the coin makes it much more valuable now," concluded the director.

"This coin is the same age as my house," commented Charlie.

After everyone had taken turns examining it, I asked if I might see it, too.

"All right, group, if you don't mind . . ."

I looked at the prize and placed it in an aluminum container before putting it into my bag. It would be mine for such a short time, to ponder over and proudly display, and then give to Jake or Ed for them to record and preserve for posterity.

Later that day my husband, who was on vacation, came to pick me up. He had dropped me off at the site on his way to play golf at the Hannastown course a few miles down the road.

I could tell even from a distance that it was Wayne strolling over toward me. He has always liked bright-colored clothes—the peacock in our family— and I could spot him immediately by the chromatic violence of his orange and yellow plaid slacks.

When Wayne at last reached the square where I was working, he asked with a winsome smile: "Well, did you find anything exciting?"

"Did I ever!" I exclaimed. "Wait until you hear what I unearthed. I had no sooner picked up the mattock than I began to discover all kinds of artifacts."

"Good," he said. "You can tell me about it on the way home."

As we walked over to the car, after putting away my equipment, he told me what his day had been like. Wayne was just as exhilarated as I was.

"I really hit one into the air with my nine iron," he said motioning with his hands held high.

"Is that so?" said I. "I lifted a lot of turf, too. But what was underneath was even more remarkable. At first all I found was bone and many pieces of iron. And even remains of charred wood. The ground was red, so I knew that it had been burned at one time. It was a rubbish pit. The hole must have been at least a foot deep."

"Uhuh. That's interesting," he murmured. "On the first hole, I knocked the ball on with a four wood, but on the second I had to use a nine iron. And I burned the hole with that one!"

"Then I found a pin," I said going on. "A copper-like straight pin. I've been wanting to find one for so long now. I almost mistook it for a blade of grass. And not only that, but also a man's tie-stick pin. You know, they're really in fashion today. Only women are wearing them instead of men."

"No kidding," said he. "I bladed the ball and still knocked it right up to the pin. Now our scores were tied. I used that same stick on the next hole, too," he said gesturing with his hands.

"Kirke and Helen were out here today," I remarked. "Kirke told me about the rattlesnake flag that they're going to put up on the site some time in the future."

"Is that right? While my partner was out in the woods killing a few snakes, I hit one on the green and it rolled up to the flag."

"Then I found a brass thimble and a wedding ring. They were both green from being in the ground all those years. Oh, and a large musket ball, too. But it was rough and looked as though it had been shot from a gun," I added.

"Really," he mumbled. "On the next shot I holed it out. The green there wasn't as rough and the ball rolled right in."

I told him about all the ceramics that were in my square. "One was the largest potsherd I've discovered so far. It was part of a cup and had a hand-painted bird on it. But the glaze was all chipped and it was hard to tell exactly what the rest of the design was."

"I had an eagle on the 10th hole and on the 15th I chipped it close to the cup," he said intensively. "Had to hand it to my partner, though. He had a birdie on the last hole."

'Uhuh," I replied with feigned interest. "But the most important find of the entire day was when I uncovered a coin. My very first. It was a silver Spanish one worth two reales. And wait until you hear what the date was: 1776," I said breathlessly.

"Great," said he swinging his arms once more. "On the last hole I two-putted for a score of 76. Not my usual score," he said modestly. "But wow, what a game!" he concluded.

"This was certainly my lucky day, too," I said.

"Really," he questioned, turning to look at me for the first time. "What did you find?"

"Oh, all kinds of interesting things," I said, half lost in thought. "How was your game? Did you have a good score?"

He was still staring at me now. "What's the matter? Weren't you listening? Oh well, that's par for the course!"

And I just kept on walking—to the beat of a different drum.

9 • ROCK OF AGES

As narrower grows the earthly vale,
The circle widens in the sky.
These are the fragments that remain,
But those are flowers that bloom on high.
OLIVER WENDELL HOLMES

The autumn tang was in the air again, and the foliage was more beautiful than I had ever remembered from years past. There is a certain emotion that one experiences at this time that surpasses description. The sky is a brilliant blue and one can sense something different about the days even before the season is officially upon us.

No doubt Helen Hunt Jackson had this same feeling when she wrote the lines:

O suns and clouds and fields of June
And flowers of June together,
Ye cannot rival for one hour
October's bright blue weather.

I was on my way to the site one particular afternoon, but not for the purpose of digging. My friend Eileen and I were about to pick up a most delightful person. There was a "young" octogenarian living in our town who had become a legend in her own time—a retired school teacher, still active in Girl Scout leadership, and living in an early log house.

She knew the history and folklore of this valley well, and in truth, was a part of it herself. Everyone who knew her loved her, and by all—young and old alike—she was endearingly referred to as "Miss Bessie."

We came in sight of the log house that has for years been a landmark to the residents of this community. I parked the car under a gigantic horse chestnut tree in the driveway, and Eileen and I got out. This was our first meeting with Miss Bessie. We had talked about doing this for a long time. And now at last we were at the doorstep, with a plate of homemade cookies, looking forward to an interesting afternoon conversing with the local historian about the folklore of our town. Considering her age, we had decided not to wait any longer with our decision to meet her. Too many times in life we put off the things that we talk about doing, and discover to our dismay that it is too late. Then we are sorry for our delay. But for once we made it in time.

Miss Bessie was at the door, expecting our visit. And what an interesting and enlightening one it was. In the course of our conversation she expressed a desire to see the excavations at Hanna's Town. We had one problem—trying to find a time when we could all get together to go. My friend's schedule and my own were busy enough, but they were nothing compared to Miss Bessie's. She walked briskly over to her desk and flipped open her social calendar. And on the hours that we were free, she had something booked solid for the next two weeks. No grass was going to grow under her feet!

At last we did manage to find a day when we could get together again, and we stopped by her house at the time we had set. This afternoon Miss Bessie had something for us— buckeyes that she had gathered from around the huge tree that shades her property. We were to use them for making fall decorations and nut wreaths for Christmas.

On the way to Hanna's Town Miss Bessie told us interesting stories and anecdotes about this area—how an early settler with the surname of McIlduff (later changed to Duff, an ancestor of a Pennsylvania governor), living in the near vicinity, had seen and smelled the smoke from a distance when Hanna's Town was burned by Indians and British two hundred years ago. He was on his way to the county courthouse (in Robert Hanna's tavern) to file a deed. Realizing what had happened, he quickly returned in fear for the safety of the family he had left behind. According to the folklore, on the way back he came upon the mutilated bodies of neighbors and friends he had spoken to only a short time before, when starting on his journey.

To hear her relate the story, it all sounds very real—as though it had just happened yesterday. "When he reached the crest of the hill," she said, "there was no sign of the Indians, except his home in flames on the opposite ridge. Not a word did he utter, but, his brow knit with worry, he rushed down the hill. In desperation he stumbled into the clearing when out of the woodlands came a cry: 'John!' You can imagine his great relief. His wife and son had hid in the woods, safe from the tomahawks of the savages. The legend is that when he heard the good news, he gave thanks to God on the very spot, and later donated that land for a church to be built on the same location. Today in the village of Export a later church stands there, and in an adjoining cemetery is the grave of John McIlduff."

Before long we were approaching a little graveyard on the right side of the road that led down into the valley at Hanna's Town. Since Miss Bessie was anxious to read the epitaphs, I stopped the car and the three of us got out.

Then quite suddenly—before we knew what she was doing—Miss Bessie was down on her knees beside a tombstone, vigorously pulling out a cherry sapling that had started to shoot its way up the side of the marker.

"We must get rid of this," she exclaimed, "or before long it will be cracking the stone in two." Needless to say, the tree was removed, then and there.

When we returned to the car, it took us only a few minutes to go down over the hill and into the parking lot of the courthouse farm.

My friend Pete came over to greet us. Overcoming his shyness, he was becoming more loquacious every day. Pete was so frequently at the site that I looked forward to his bubbling enthusiasm as he welcomed me on each arrival. And if I didn't see him at first, I would no sooner be out of the car than I would hear his voice cheerfully calling:

"Hi, Helene. Did you bring Brigette with you today?"

On the rare occasions when Pete wasn't there, I knew that it would just be a matter of time before I would see him coming down the old Forbes Road on his bicycle, waving and calling my name, eager as ever to show me his latest discovery at Hanna's Town or from some Indian site nearby. Pete seemed to know where many of the old Indian camps were located in that area, and had an uncanny way of finding interesting and unusual artifacts. His younger brother Denny, who came out with him from time to time, was also good at this. He had found a rare presidential button in a field neighboring the site. It was from George Washington's inauguration and he donated it to the historical society, even though he must have had mixed emotions about relinquishing it.

(Pete always recorded and catalogued everything that he found—Jake, his mentor, had coached him well. Too many collectors of Indian artifacts, and pothunters alike, never keep records of their discoveries, and valuable information is often lost as a result. Thank goodness for those who care.)

On one such occasion Pete invited me to go along with him in search of Indian relics. It was a beautiful day and I welcomed the break from digging. A farmer had recently plowed his field not far down the road, and after getting permission from the owner, the two of us set out to walk the furrows in search of prehistoric artifacts and early ceramics.

Immediately after a field has been plowed—or even better, after it has been harrowed and had a rain—is an excellent opportunity to find Indian artifacts. And most farmers, if asked, will very willingly consent to this type of exploration on their property. About digging they are not always so generous.

One would think that after all those years, artifacts such as these would have disappeared with the constant plowing and turning over of the soil by diligent searchers, or by accidental finds while sowing the fields. But as far as the points are concerned, there were so many of these prehistoric ones on the ground at the time of early settlement that the pioneers began to use them in making their gun flints. And to this day there are still many to be found. There must have been thousands of them scattered about everywhere when this country was first discovered.

After this, Pete and the children and I took other historic

excursions to neighboring sites of interest. There was the plantation of Colonel John Proctor, the leader of Westmoreland's First Battalion which carried the famous rattlesnake flag during the Revolutionary War. Here, in this area, also had lived Jeremiah Lochry, whose company in 1781 gathered at Hanna's Town and traveled down the Ohio to meet George Rogers Clark and to make plans to subdue the Indians. But the ill-fated campaign failed. And many of its members were killed.

Farther along the highway stood a picturesque girl's school—St. Xavier's, the oldest Roman Catholic academy in Western Pennsylvania. One of the nuns very graciously gave us a tour of the historic buildings which were soon to be razed, much to our dismay. Near the chapel she showed us the approximate location where Fort Shippen had once stood—another refuge among the chain of frontier forts in this section of the country.

Then there was Fort Allen, constructed in 1774—the same year as Hanna's Town's garrison. But the only thing left standing there now was an old Lutheran church with an early cemetery. This is known as Harrold's place, since many of its first settlers belonged to this German family. And Pete was a descendant of one of them.

In the front yard of the church is a stone marker with the names of eighty pioneers who had petitioned for the fort to be built. A short distance away were a weather beaten log house and barn that had withstood the storms and "progress" of the times.

Surrounding these buildings was a modern housing development which would eventually swallow up the last remaining evidence of the little frontier settlement. Shortly after our visit the old structures were demolished. It was unfortunate, because early landmarks help to keep us in touch with the past. They give us a sense of continuity and perspective. And this is important in our day when change seems to be the only constant.

Perhaps I have more than my share of a passion for early American life, but the simple charm of that age-old ivy-covered log house and its humble surroundings of an apple orchard and stone springhouse, somehow have more appeal than the austere-looking grounds circling the last remains. The contrast is great. But in the name of profit and progress, the trees go along with the historic buildings. And the bulldozers continue to erase our heritage from the landscape. Unless the appreciation for the early craftsmen's architecture becomes more widespread, many more of these unpretentious buildings of similar charm will be destroyed.

To continue, there was Miller's blockhouse where some of the residents were either killed or taken prisoner at the time of the attack on Hanna's Town. On a hillside, not far away from this location, is a lone marker of stone designating the grave of an early settler and his child who were tomahawked by the Indians as they were being taken captive from Millers.

We stopped and read the inscription at our feet:

Joseph Brownlee, I Lieut.
13 Pa. Regt. Rev. War.
July 13, 1782

Life was horrendous for these pioneers when the Indians were on the rampage. But in all fairness, what must the Indians have felt in those days, when their land and hunting grounds were taken over by these new pioneer families expanding the frontier? (History does not often record the number of Indians scalped by white men.) Their villages had been here long before the earliest settlers.

Pete and I had the opportunity to visit one of these ancient Indian sites being excavated several miles from Hanna's Town near the village of Bouquet (named after Colonel Henry Bouquet, who fought victoriously at the Battle of Bushy Run in 1763 and made peace with the Indians a year later). Only this dig was carried out in a manner to which we were not accustomed. Here everything was excavated in a given area at one time, without the benefit of sifting the dirt inch by inch as we do at our site.

Once the top soil was removed and the yellow clay bottom exposed, this layer was then meticulously plotted on maps as to where the post-molds and pits were. These features had been carefully excavated and sifted.

Prehistoric archeology is different in this respect from our method of digging. These early remains are not easily spotted in a limited area. Usually there is a bewildering mass of post-molds (many from the picket structure of their huts), and therefore the safest way is to clear a fairly large horizontal section before digging systematically.

Kirke was in charge of those excavations, and one day he had brought over his crew of volunteers to visit Hanna's Town. So we had decided to return the compliment. This exchange of information and knowledge is invaluable—an experience which textbooks alone cannot provide.

Meanwhile, back at the site—where Pete was more often than not—I always looked forward to hearing about his latest discoveries as he would come over to the car to greet me on each arrival. And today was no exception. After the introductions were all made, he took something from his pocket. "Wait until you see what I found!" he cried. Pete held up a copper disk and we examined it carefully.

"It's the earliest coin I've dug up so far. Look at the date—1730!" he chortled. "I can't wait to see Jake's face when he sees this one!" (Jake, later, truly did express his pleasure and delight in what Pete had discovered. And Pete's face reflected Jake's.)

In no time at all Pete and Miss Bessie were talking like old friends who hadn't seen each other for years. There was certainly no generation gap here. In spite of the difference in years, Miss Bessie was just as enthusiastic and interested in what Pete was saying as he was in her stories. Eileen and I (who could hardly get a word in edgewise) gladly took a back seat in the conversation and enjoyed listening while the two of them rambled on.

After we gave our companion a tour of the site and showed her the field museum, I looked at Eileen's watch. (Never could get used to wearing one of my own—always depending upon someone else to tell me how far the day has progressed.) According to the time, our children would soon be coming home from school, so we had to leave. As the three of us turned to go, Miss Bessie said wistfully, looking across the field where the excavations lay: "What I wouldn't give to dig at a place like this."

When we reached Miss Bessie's log house in the shade of the great horse-chestnut tree, we said goodbye and I wondered if I would ever see her again.

Shortly after this adventure I picked up the newspaper and read that Miss Bessie had died. She was 84 years young. To know her was to love her. And may the cherry trees never disturb her resting place.

10 • CONVERSATIONS AT THE SPRING

The earth never tires,
The earth is rude, silent, incomprehensible at first . . .
. . . .
Be not discouraged, keep on, there are divine things well envelop'd.
WALT WHITMAN

It was one of those unbelievably hot days "not fit for man nor beast," and in spite of the scorching heat, there were a few die-hards working on the site.

Before starting in my square, I smoothed some lotion on my skin for protection from the rays of the sun, paying special attention to my arms. My mother used to say: "You can always tell a woman's age by her elbows." And, being a typical female in this respect, I wasn't about to give out any secrets.

Some of the volunteers had erected a sun shelter from scraps of lumber and a tarpaulin. This helped somewhat in overcoming the problem of the heat. I looked down at my little dog. Already she was panting from being so hot, and after giving me a reproachful look, got up and trotted away, seeking "coolth." Anyone who works out here in this sizzling temperature has to be crazy, I told myself.

But Kipling's words prodded me on.

The cure for this ill is not to sit still,
Or frowst with a book by the fire;
But to take a large hoe and a shovel also,
And dig till you gently perspire.

Brigette had caused enough havoc in one morning's time.

92

For days Jake had been diligently working around a bone, using painstaking care not to dislodge it from its original location and keeping it in place for photographing. After brushing the last particle of dirt away and leaving the artifact neatly to rest, he rose from his kneeling position and stretched. A few minutes later he returned to the site after talking to some nearby diggers about their progress. At that moment he spied my playful mutt running along gleefully with a bone in her mouth, looking for a good hiding place in the dirt. I shall never forget the look on his face until he realized that it was an old soup bone abandoned by Leroy, the caretaker's dog, a few days previously.

Shortly after this episode a visitor walked over and broke the ice (wish there were some!) with: "Oh, there's that German dog with the French name."

"You must have been talking with my children over by the barn," I replied, still thinking about Brigette and how she had fooled Jake.

"Yes, they were having a great time with their pet," he agreed. And how well I knew exactly what he meant, for never was there a more beloved dog with five siblings lavishing on it such enthusiastic affection as only children can offer.

"How did you get interested in Hanna's Town?" he asked, after introducing himself.

Thinking how I had always been keenly fascinated by history and archeology alike, just as my mother before me had been, but at the same time not wanting to go into any lengthy elaboration of the subject, I merely stated:

"Well, it's certainly closer than Egypt!" And let it go at that.

"Tell me," he went on, "is there any place where I can see some of the artifacts that have been dug up here—that is, besides sticks, stones, and bones?" I could tell by the way he was watching me sift the soil that he was not impressed. Momentarily I was not finding anything of much interest.

"Well," I answered with a sense of amusement. "As a matter of fact there is. And you're closer to them than you think."

"That so?" he said smiling and making himself more comfortable.

"Yes," I said, almost laughing. "You're sitting on it."

Startled by this revelation the man stood up and looked down at the slab of cement that he had rested upon and discovered it to be the roof of the underground field museum banked into the ground.

"You're welcome to go in and look around," I said. And with a grin he disappeared underneath the ground to see the treasures of Hanna's Town.

It wasn't long until Harriet and Walter, a very pleasant couple who live in the farmhouse and are the caretakers for the site, walked over to where I was digging. Harriet is a jolly person who is a constant delight to be around, and she was on her way to see her pride and joy—the garden. (She, too, has turned up many an interesting artifact with her spade.)

This year some of the volunteers were imbued with the urge to plant a garden as well. Only we sowed our seeds on two of the spoils piles, located on various strategic spots on the county property. They were only temporary, for periodically the dirt was hauled away. But not before our plants were through the growing season.

Pete had erected several signs on the top of the spoils piles. One he called the King's Garden after King George III who was the ruling figure of England at the time of Hanna's Town, and another he called the Queen's Garden, in honor of the sovereign's consort, Charlotte. Pete had planted tomatoes, lettuce, beans, and even corn, while one of the other volunteers had less judiciously sown pumpkins. (Recently some of our members planted an honest-to-goodness vegetable and herb garden behind the courthouse-tavern.)

"Hey, Helene," called Pete as he walked over to join us. "Your pumpkins are getting ripe—and by the way, you owe me one. A vine of yours has choked my tomato plant." (One of the disadvantages of a small garden.)

"O.K., Pete, pick out a good one," I agreed wholeheartedly. Then he and Harriet went to inspect her harvest.

"You know, Walter," I said after they had left, "all the times that I've been out here, I keep wanting to ask you about something and never seem to remember until I am halfway home. I have noticed that throughout this property there are large brick posts that one would likely see at an entrance to some estate. But they're just standing as lone markers on various places in fields and along the road. What were they used for?"

"Oh, Judge Steel, who had a special feeling for this place—being the first seat of justice—had these built a long time ago when he was living here. There's not as many now as there used to be—over the years they've slowly disappeared.

"Wherever there was a gate, there were brick posts like the ones you see today on the property. Over across the field," he said, pointing beyond the barn, "the judge planted a pine grove, made a driveway, and built two more brick posts, walls, and a gate. This was where his mansion house was to be, but he died before the ground was ever broken."

Now as I looked I could see the trees and the lonely entranceway to a long-forgotten desire. I couldn't help but feel a bit sad, for along with the happiness in my own fulfillment, here stood the remnants of a lost dream.

I realized even more that there was not only a story to be told concerning the old Hanna's Town, but in later history as well. And I thought—just as the song goes—"O bla de. O bla da"—life goes on. Someday others may peer into the rubble of our own lives and wonder, too.

During a dig, from time to time, I would look up from what I was doing and rest my eyes on the surrounding landscape. On this particular occasion I glanced across the far field to the north where Walter had pointed out the lone grove of pine and solitary brick gate posts, and my attention became focused on some county workmen planting tree seedlings in the distance. As I gazed in their direction, I suddenly saw a jeep taking a cross-country shortcut through the field and heading toward me, leaving a cloud of summer dust behind. I got up and stretched my legs, standing fascinated, as closer and closer it came.

Presently when the vehicle reached me, a man got out and walked quickly over, as though he had a quest to fulfill. He was a handsome man, and topping off his tall frame was a yellow hard hat. Underneath no artist could have missed observing the beautiful, brilliant shade of his china blue eye.

"Hello," he said.

"Hi," said I. And in the course of our conversation I found him to be both interesting and charming. I was no longer conscious of the fact that he had but one eye. He obviously was aware of the Hanna's Town project and his mission was to bring me two flint arrow points that he had just uncovered while working in the field. They were in perfect condition—one being gray, and the other of a reddish shade.

"Here, I'd like to donate these to your organization," he said, upon finding that I belonged to the Westmoreland County Historical Society. After thanking him, I thought: There are so very many nice people on this earth—in all walks of life.

The sun was soon directly overhead, and my stomach was well aware of that time of the day. I took the lunch that I had prepared before starting out and walked over to the spring to eat in the shade. My friend brought his lunch over and sat down on the steps under the great branches, too—the two of us fighting off the sudden charge of dogs and cats taking a special interest in our food.

This spring, that knows no ceasing, was the source of refreshment where people had congregated ever since the beginning of civilization here, and perhaps for aborigines, many centures before that. What discussions must have taken place on these premises, I would never know, but could well imagine.

Possibly two hundred years ago a group of men and women stood here and talked of the oncoming Revolutionary War, border raids or even the Hanna's Town Resolves, which were formulated on this very soil. From history I recalled that here was the place where the frontiersmen of Westmoreland had gathered to draw up their own protest against England's unjust treatment of the Colonies—a forerunner of the Declaration of Independence. Standing on the same earth where the settlers had their rendezvous, I picked up one of the small stones at my feet and held it in my hand for a brief moment. Perhaps someone from another century had fondled this pebble also. As we conversed my thoughts kept reverting to that period years ago. I could almost sense the presence of the early pioneers.

The meeting had taken place only four weeks after the British had fired on Lexington. And the crowd was so great that they *did* have to meet out under the trees of the wilderness—for there was no room in the inn. Robert Hanna's courthouse-tavern was filled to capacity.

I could visualize the excitement and rowdiness of that hectic spring day. Voices that were stilled long ago must have shouted such exclamations as: "Our men have been murdered! . . . The stamp tax won't be the only thing we'll oppose! . . . We'll make our own laws! . . . And have our own flag—one that will make the Redcoats stand up and take notice!"

And I envisioned Arthur St. Clair, the chief author of the resolves and perhaps the most influential man in this territory at that time, standing here before the mob, trying to appease them with: "Men, let us finish our resolutions. We can feel some consolation . . for they are meeting in Pittsburgh for the same purpose today. There is strength in numbers."

St. Clair concluded his reading of the resolves:

"At a general meeting of the inhabitants of the County of Westmoreland, held at Hanna's Town the 16th of May, 1775, for taking into consideration the very alarming situation of this country, occasioned by the dispute with Great Britain . . . *Resolved unanimously,* That there is no reason to doubt but the same system of tyranny and oppression will (should it meet with success in the Massachusetts Bay) be extended to every other part of America; it is, therefore, become the indispensible duty of every American, of every man who has any publick virtue or love of his Country, or any bowels for posterity, by every means which God has put in his power, to resist and oppose the execution of it; that for us, we will be ready to oppose it with our lives and fortunes."

And these people truly meant it! In the words of Patrick Henry, "Give me liberty, or give me death." Perhaps nowhere else in the colonies were the people more ready and willing to go to war against Britain. For many were rambunctious Scotch-Irish, who had known persecution in their fatherland and who had just recently come through the terror of Indian uprisings, and directly blamed England for the troubles on the frontier.

The next day, following the adoption of the resolutions, St. Clair became apprehensive and wrote in a letter to a friend: "God grant an end may be speedily put to any necessity for such proceedings. I doubt their utility, and am almost as much afraid of success in this contest as of being vanquished."

No doubt there were many discussions over the issue. And where more appropriately than at a tavern—or even outside around a spring? Suddenly Arthur St. Clair and a friend stood beside me, engaged in conversation.

(St. Clair) "Have no doubt. We are falling on long and difficult days. The Indians are paid by the British and will always be in the British interest. There is no question that partisans will use these troubles as a device to press the Virginia claim to our land. The fort here could not hold out long against a concentrated attack and it is doubtful if even Fort Pitt could withstand a lengthy siege."

(Friend) 'There's a great deal in what you say, Colonel St. Clair. And I wonder if it might not be the wiser course to give up our efforts here, as some have already done, and return to the Great Valley, at least until this conflict ends . . and this would probably mean forever."

(St. Clair) "Indeed it would mean forever. There is little doubt, now the die is cast, that things will go much farther between Britain and our colonies. Our resolves declared a continued loyalty to King George and said nothing of becoming an independent nation. But you can see with half an eye that this is a pretense. Our revolt has gone too far to be settled by a mere change of parties. Where we are now blaming Parliament we will soon be laying the blame on the Crown as well."

(Friend) "And truly, his Majesty is as much at fault, allowing himself to become a mere puppet in the hands of a Tory Parliament."

(St. Clair) "Then we are agreed that it will be war, and

one in which we will be hard put to preserve both lives and liberty in the West."

(Friend) "What other choice have we?"

(St. Clair) "None but to stand our ground as we have declared, and oppose this tyranny. We both know the situation in which our colonies find themselves. Already overcrowded, and pinned down to the narrow plains between this long mountain range and the sea. We are hemmed in on the north by Canada, which is still too much involved with working out its French problems to be concerned with ours. On the south the French and Spaniards prevent any effort to expand."

(Friend) "Could a nation long endure penned in, in such a fashion?"

(St. Clair) "As you well know, it would not. Either we keep a foothold on this side of the mountains, or all our efforts will have been in vain even if we win a temporary victory."

(Friend) "Then . . .?"

(St. Clair) "The future of our nation—if we are to be a nation—hangs on this spearhead of settlement in the West."

(Friend) "And if we allow the Tories to take this area, rest assured, we will not be able to get it back."

(St. Clair) "But, on the other hand, if we can maintain this, all the great plains at least to the Mississippi, will lie before us as soon as peace can be achieved."

(Friend) "Then your counsel is . . . ?"

(St. Clair) "Not my counsel—our necessity. On these slim outposts of settlement stand all we seem destined to fight for."

(Friend) "I agree with your position, Colonel St. Clair. We have a rendezvous here with destiny. And with you I cast in my lot. Here, on and for this beginning of room to expand, we will offer and if need be, give our lives, our fortunes, and our sacred honor."

(St. Clair) "Amen. And may the Lord of Hosts aid us in our endeavor."

These people had begun something too great ever to be stopped. The march of destiny in America was on its way.

*   *   *   *   *   *

The voices of the past were no longer there and only an occasional breeze disturbed the leaves above our heads. As the county workman and I sat eating our lunch, I imagined less earth-shaking discussions that probably took place at this eternal spring. Such conversations as the weather, crops, food prices, gossip—or even what the two of us were talking about at the moment.

"Oh, so you have teenagers, too," he was saying. And one could talk for hours on that subject alone. But we both had "miles to go," so after we had finished our meal, he went back to his work and I to mine.

When I had returned to my square, Pete wandered over from the other side of the road where he had been working in a pit area.

"Have ya ever done any water flotation before, Helene?" he asked. Before I had a chance to reply Pete said, "Come on and I'll show ya' how it's done." Evidently Jake had introduced him to a new type of discovery. Not wanting to miss anything, I followed. We took a screen and a bucket of dirt with us and made our way across the field to the barn. There, a stream of water from the spring flowed from a pipe into a cement trough that was once used for the farm animals. I was about to learn a new method in discovering artifacts.

In archeology, water flotation is a good way to find minute evidence of what earlier civilizations had, and otherwise used. Along with this even the percentage of what was consumed years ago can be determined. The microscopic study of pollen grains and other remnants of foodstuff reveals much information along this line.

As any paleobotanist would tell us, pollen has a very long life, particularly if preserved in damp soil—and especially in peat. Not all pollen germinates but instead much lies dormant in the earth and becomes overlaid with successive layers of soil, each containing later pollen grains. Under the lens of a microscope one can tell the nature and characteristics of trees, grasses, and plant life years ago, and sometimes date levels by the plant migrations. Also, earlier environments can be determined. A preponderance of oak and elm pollen suggests a warm, moist region, while pine and birch are evidence of dry, cold surroundings.

Perhaps some day I may have an opportunity to study the pollen under a microscope. But for now it was interesting to find visible seed and discover the dietary habits of people who lived on this earth before our time.

As we talked, Pete emptied the bucket of dirt into the screen and then lowered the whole works beneath the water. The earth soon washed out through the mesh and left a coarse sediment of tiny pebbles on the bottom and black wood ashes floating on the surface. It was at that moment that Pete started to pick up small objects from the screen.

"What's that?" I asked dumbfounded, for I certainly couldn't see anything but sticks and stones.

"Fish scales, egg shells, seeds, and tiny bones that, surprisingly enough, do not decompose in the earth. And look, even a straight pin that someone had missed," he said triumphantly. (On rare occasions, artifacts do have a way of showing up where they're not supposed to be. When this happens, it is usually due to carelessness on the part of the screener or perhaps a novice at work. But to err is human, and the spoils pile is no exception. In order to help compensate for this, it is a good idea to check this area frequently, and especially after a rain. However, pins are easily lost—being minute by nature—even by the most experienced excavators. At times they escape unnoticed through the first screening process. But by using the water flotation method they can be recovered in features where they would most likely occur.

To me it was extremely interesting that after all these years the earth not only held artifacts of civilizations centuries before our time, but also still retained traces of what the inhabitants had eaten.

To learn something about a group of people, one of the first things to study is their environment. And this includes what sort of vegetation they had to deal with and what their wild or domesticated animals were at that time.

The identification of animals is relatively simple, for the bones can be distinguished. And this may give clues as to the natural vegetation around them. For example, pigs graze in forests whereas sheep and cattle like open countryside.

Household habits show up, too. One of the volunteers had uncovered a pewter spoon from Foreman's tavern site with the initials S.C.F. on it—a plausible explanation being that it could have belonged to the innkeeper's wife, Sarah. Strangely enough, there was egg shell still clinging to it. Someone had not done the dishes! But maybe the owner was taken by surprise when the raiders were attacking Hanna's Town. I have been known to leave tableware in the sink for a lesser excuse than an Indian foray!

11 • THIS OLD HOUSE

Be through my lips to unawakened earth
The trumpet of a prophecy! O, Wind,
If Winter comes, can Spring be far behind?
PERCY BYSSHE SHELLEY

There is no season quite so marvelous as spring. Poets have extolled its splendor ever since the beginning of history. Shiny new-formed leaves have not as yet had a chance to accumulate summer dust from country roads and highways, and the fragrance of the earth that is present in the air rekindles the spirit within child and adult alike. Even the birds sing praises to the newness of life in the symphony of spring. For a brief time our ears become deafened to the tumult of the earth—hearing, instead, an eternal melody renewed each spring. And the world falls in love once again.

Such a day it was when I reached the hill overlooking the Hanna's Town site. It was early. No one had yet arrived, not even Pete.

Today I was about to start a new square across the road in the plowed field that Jake and Ed had recently surveyed with the aid of a transit and marked off into plots. I found the key in its usual place and opened the door to the shed to get my equipment for digging.

This was a cue for the numerous cats on the premises to jump up on my car, looking very much like hood ornaments, and making themselves quite at home. If you don't remember to close all the windows—I discovered through experience—they will take over the inside as well. And when you kneel to dig, one has the habit of taking you by surprise—leaping on your back when you least expect it.

After gathering what was needed, I picked up Brigette and placed her in the wheelbarrow along with everything else. Although she enjoyed riding in it, her wistful look told me at a glance that she would have preferred to stay behind and chase the cats around the barnyard. But when we reached the other side of the highway, I let her down and she was content to follow along with me.

There was a large unexplored field lying before me, undisturbed, except for annual plowing, since the 1770s. Over the years people of all ages had walked its furrows in search of projectile points and other artifacts. But it had never been systematically excavated down to the depth of its layered occupation—in the Petrie manner—until now.

Brigette was off tearing across the field in zig-zag fashion, sniffing every inch of the aromatic ground. I walked over to the stakes, selected a square, and began. There was a whir of wings overhead. The dog had just startled a meadowlark from the protective grass.

Taking the horizontal end of the mattock, I loosened the sod in my square. And after shaking each piece bit by bit to be sure there were no artifacts in it, I placed the turf in the wheelbarrow to be discarded on a spoils pile nearby.

After so long I began to feel the effect of the morning sun. I glanced up, but for a fraction of a second—for it was bright and there was not a trace of a cloud in sight. Looking away, my eyes found concentric circles and brilliant spots from the rays superimposed over whatever I saw. Somewhat dizzy, I soon regained my former vision and went on with my work, scraping the soil a little at a time.

Nothing much had come in view in the two hours that I had been there. This square was quite different from what I was used to working in across the way where one found all kinds of road materials, ceramics, bits and pieces of bricks, and glass.

Here the only items I had uncovered so far were of a military nature—bullets and gun flints (both gray ones imported from England, and amber from France—since foreign flint was superior to local resources). A little redware turned up and not much of anything else.

Another thing I noted was the difference in the depth of the occupied layers. This was shallow compared to the squares that had been excavated across the road. Here I had gone down only twelve inches and already the lighter shade of the bottom clay was commencing to show.

In the last bucketful of dirt that I had screened, a buff colored marble appeared. It was typical of what children played with before glass ones were manufactured—dug as clay, molded and fired in a kiln or oven. This is a simple toy that young people have used since the beginning of humankind. Only the material had changed—not the design.

Just then I felt a breeze, a welcome relief in heat. My hair blew around and into my eyes. There were a few clouds starting to gather in the sky. The sound of a door banging shut startled me. I looked over to the crossroads and saw the ancient, weathered house, its logs concealed under brown clapboards. That was strange, I thought—the door to the little dark building was open and swinging back and forth. The impact of another gust of wind made it slam again, and then rock freely back and forth on its hinges. Usually the house was kept locked at all times.

Suddenly a voice from behind took me by surprise.

"Hello," it said.

Still kneeling, I turned around and was face to face with a young girl. She was in her bare feet and a lock of chestnut brown hair hung down in her face. It was unusual that she had such a tan so early in the season —for she was as "brown as a summer berry" as my grandmother used to say.

The girl said hello again, and by now I had regained enough composure to respond. She didn't seem inclined to leave, and presently sat down beside me.

"Where do you live?" I inquired, wondering where in the world she had popped up from, for when I had turned around it seemed as if she appeared out of nowhere.

My little friend pointed in the direction of the abandoned log house. Although she was looking at the weather-beaten structure, I knew that she surely must be referring to the farm house beyond, just out of sight over the hill.

And then turning to me she asked: "What are you doing?"

"I'm hunting for artifacts—things that were left here by the early settlers at the time before the village of Hanna's Town was burned by the Indians."

She didn't say anything but seemed to have a strange look in her eyes. I went on: "You know—broken dishes, tableware, old jewelry and . . . Look, here." I motioned for her to see what was in my bag. "I want to show you something I just found."

Remembering my latest discovery, I reached into the paper sack that contained everything that I had unearthed that day.

"Here," I said, "is a clay marble, handmade and used by someone living perhaps two hundred years ago."

She took it and held it in the palm of her hand.

I continued to scrape the soil with a trowel as she watched every move I made. I was at the bottom now, when suddenly a dark, round circle appeared in the yellow clay. Soon another one followed when I uncovered the section about a foot away from the first feature.

"Look," I said. "These are post-molds." I explained to her that when a post is driven into the ground and allowed to decay for a period of years, the soil will show up dark and loose from the decomposition of the wood.

"There must have been a building or a structure of some kind here at one time." I scrutinized the ground more carefully now.

Suddenly the stillness of the morning was broken with the sound of her laughter. I looked up.

"What is so funny?" I questioned.

"You silly thing," she giggled. "That's where the fort was."

That's odd, I pondered. I hadn't mentioned anything about a fort to her.

"Colonel Sinclair told us that we should have a stockade," she went on, "in case of an Indian attack. We always watched the military musters here. And people came from all over the county to see them."

Now, I knew from history that in 1774 Arthur St. Clair had indeed advised the settlers of Hanna's Town to build a fortified blockhouse for protection. It was at the same time that Lord Dunmore (John Murray), the governor of Virginia, was claiming this part of Pennsylvania for his colony on the basis that it either lay west of the boundaries granted to the Penns, or south of their proper claims.

For several years, until late in the Revolution, rival Virginia and Pennsylvania jurisdiction sought to control the region. Dr. John Connolly—agent to Lord Dunmore—raised havoc on the frontier by burning the crops, barns, and livestock. And in 1774 a group of Virginia partisans rode into Hanna's Town, broke open the jail and freed the prisoners. Later they arrested Robert Hanna and other court officials.

But how would this young girl know anything about the fort and the troubles at that time? She even talked as though she had been there.

Now from experience I knew not to question the fantasy of youth. Besides, I knew that the fort site was across the road where a bronze marker had been placed at the spring years ago, designating the approximate location.

I decided to play along with her. "How do you know for sure?" I asked in a serious tone.

"Because I watched the men build it," she replied.

What an imagination, I thought. I didn't say anything but instead just looked at her. There was something about her that was different—but just as she was about to speak again, the girl turned suddenly as if she had heard a noise.

Handing me the clay marble she jumped up and quickly, before I had a chance to say anything, headed in the direction of the weathered log house.

"Wait! Don't leave," I called almost pleadingly. "Come back, please come back."

I ran after her with Brigette following close at my heels. She turned and looked in my direction. The air rang with laughter once again. She reached the house ahead of me and disappeared inside.

By the time that I got there I was puffing like someone who had just finished a cross-country race. I stopped and leaned against the wall for a moment to catch my breath before entering.

At last I turned and grasped the rough plank door by the iron handle. For the moment all I could see was a gossamer-like maze as it swung open. I brushed away a cobweb that was hanging down in my face and obstructing my entry. When my eyes had become accustomed to the dismal interior, I felt as though I had just entered a tomb. The air was musty and thick—age-old dust clung to everything, making some objects indistinguishable.

Over in a corner I could make out a very old rocking chair. It began to sway back and forth as I stepped on the floor board that it was resting upon. I had an eerie feeling about this place and almost turned to leave. But I had seen the girl enter here and she had to be somewhere inside.

Along the far wall were indefinable items all strung together and blurred by gray cobwebs. Near these intriguing objects hung some kind of herbs which had long ago lost their fragrance and were faded by time. Close by was a string of what appeared to be Indian beads.

Slowly my eyes scanned the rest of the room. Overhead there was a loft, with steps leading up to it. I crossed the floor toward the steps. Some of the soft, rotting boards began to give way with my weight, and I had to step where the joists supported them. I looked up and began to ascend to the loft. The girl was probably trying to fool me, for I didn't hear a sound. Well, two could play this game as well as one, I thought. I'll take her by surprise. She's no doubt hiding in a corner somewhere. I would be ready for her laughter this time.

After ascending to the loft, I looked all around for my new friend. She was nowhere in sight. There were some old barrels and a horsehair trunk in the corner. I quietly walked over to them and looked inside. "Ahah!—there you are," I said expecting to find her. But they were empty.

I began to search more diligently. She had to be here. The sun filtered in through one small, dust-covered window across the room. I could tell it had not been opened in years. The cobwebs were undisturbed. There was no way that the girl could have escaped through the window. I turned and looked all around the room in puzzlement. No one was here and no one had been here in the first place. I was the only person who had entered the log house.

Brigette began to bark in the room below where I had left her. Slowly I descended to the first floor and walked out, closing the door behind me. I locked it so that the wind would no longer blow it open.

Returning to my square, I began to dig once more, this time deep in thought. I had not even asked what her name was. How foolish of me! A twig snapped behind me. "Ah, there you are," I exclaimed and wheeled around quickly. But it was not my little elusive friend after all. Instead, it was Jake. He had arrived at the site without me even hearing his car pull in the driveway—I had been so lost in thought.

"Oh," I said upon seeing who it was.

"Who did you expect?" he asked.

"No one," I hesitated. "You just took me by surprise, that's all."

I showed Jake the post-molds that I had uncovered. He got down and looked at them carefully. "There was a structure here all right," he said, rubbing his chin thoughtfully. "We'll have to follow them and determine where they go. Better leave them for now until Ed has a chance to sketch them in."

In the course of time other volunteers uncovered a trench and more post-molds within it, following it as the dimensions grew into the size of a rectangle 122 by 69 feet. Before it was completed, Jake came over to me one morning saying: "Well, Helene, do you know what you discovered?"

I swallowed hard. I had a feeling that it was something important but was half afraid to hope that it really might be . . .

"The fort," Jake said. "We have established that this was the location of the Hanna's Town stockade built in 1774."

I stood there looking at the unpretentious brown house with the log cabin underneath its weatherboards. It had stood silent throughout the years, revealing to no one the secret of the fortress site that it overlooked. And I didn't say a word to anyone about the mysterious little girl.

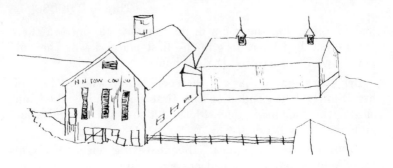

12 • ON WINGS OF TIME

All merry noise of hens astir
Or sparrows squabbling on the roof
Comes to the barn's broad open door . . .
EDMUND BLUNDEN

On this particular day I had brought a friend with me to help excavate my square. A helicopter whirred noisily over our heads. We had been watching it curiously as it hovered over us in the fort area across the road from the spring.

"I wonder if it's planning to land," Pat commented as she shielded her eyes from the sun. The ancient magnet which draws people out from their shelters on nice days was shining radiantly. Many volunteers had come to the site to work this day, hopeful of progress toward the restoration of Hanna's Town. Among them was one named Bill.

Bill had struck a pit area across the road and not hit bottom yet—not even after ten and a half feet! And for the longest time I didn't even know that someone was working down there, for he was at a level and a location that were out of view.

An earlier time, before I had an opportunity to meet him, we were digging side by side in two adjacent squares belonging to the same ten-foot section. But he never saw me, nor I him, the entire period that we were working there. When he would come out to the site to dig, I would not be present. And on the days that I was there, he was absent. When first starting to excavate my square, I always noticed that someone had gone down a layer lower than mine. But by the end of the day, my quarter was below his. The mysterious person would then come out on another occasion and gain more depth than I had.

This routine continued until we at last reached bottom, with neither one of us knowing the ghost digger next door. Then on the last day that we dug on these squares, quite by a stroke of coincidence or the law of averages, we came to Hanna's Town on the same afternoon and finished, reaching hardpan at about the same time. Thus we met and became acquainted. As we compared the artifacts from our squares it was exciting to see that many of them were of the same kind and could be pieced together. We had almost enough shards for a complete stoneware crock.

Working in a square a short distance away from Bill was a husband and wife team. They were new at the site, but with the amount of time they were spending here, would soon be catching up to some of the rest of us. Both were employed, and by two different companies, but they arranged their vacation schedules so that they could continue excavating together. And this is all volunteer work!

I happened to overhear one of them say, "I don't know what is wrong with me. Everyone else seems to find pins except me." Shades of my first summer of digging! He sounded very discouraged and I remembered how I had felt in the same situation a few years ago.

"Don't worry," I called reassuringly. "You'll find one before you know it." But he just shook his head, not believing for one minute that he would.

As I got up to stretch my legs, my eyes took in the surroundings. There had been many changes over the years. *Tempus fugit*—the seasons are as short-lived as a crocus in spring.

And so many things had happened in the meantime. All of the fort area had been dug out—and it just seemed like yesterday that we had begun to follow the post-molds and trench where the palisade had once stood. Overhead was a replica of the famed rattlesnake flag; and beyond, a 50-star American banner. The site was now nationally recognized as a historic landmark, and was on the National Register of

Historic Places. A huge sandstone boulder nearby marĸs the location of Hanna's Town.

Along with the additions there had been some subtractions, too. The little spring house, post-dating Hanna's Town, was now gone— removed from the premises with its foundation and the surrounding earth excavated and sifted for artifacts. The enormous white barn with the words, "Hanna's Town Courthouse Farm," was no longer there. It had been removed for the same reason. The building belonged to a period later than the 1700s and it, too, had to go.

The day the barn came down will long be remembered. When I arrived at the site, the wrecking crew was already there. While the action was taking place, some county workmen were widening the road. My square was located in a strategic place for watching all that was going on—right between the barn and the highway.

I had mixed emotions about that barn. The children had become acquainted with a white owl that had lived under its roof for a number of years. And although I knew that the structure had to be razed, the thought of that owl, along with all the barn swallows and pigeons losing their homes and young, gave me a strange feeling inside.

Standing with spade in hand like one of Grant Wood's characters, I watched as the gigantic demolition crane took another chunk out of the barn. With each jolt, the old familiar landmark, which up until now had defied the years, shook from side to side, as though it were gelatin. And when the wrecker came to the roof, the slate crumbled and slid, crashing to the ground in a million pieces.

And then—just as the huge metal jaws and teeth of the monster started to lift off the cupola on top, the friendly white owl flew out and circled around the barn a few times before flapping its wings across the field to the pine trees in the distance. She had waited until the very last minute before she had to abandon her home. Now the sparrows, barn swallows, and pigeons alike, were circling round and round in desperation wondering what would become of their nests, eggs, and newly hatched young.

How can I explain it? Something came over me quite suddenly. At the same time the entire roof of the barn came down, just as an elderly gentleman walked over to me. He had been quietly watching the demolition for some time now.

"I think I'm going to cry," he murmured.

Wiping my eyes, I looked in surprise in his direction.

"That was my barn they're tearing down," he said. "I used to live here and many a day I can remember entering those unwieldy doors to milk the cows and tend the horses. I can still see all those cattle over the years assuming their solemn places one by one in their stalls.

"Cobwebs and dust," he said reminiscing, "the smell of apples and hay. The barn was old, but not strange."

I agreed with him as he went on: "The missus and I just happened to be passing by, when we saw what they were doing." I could see the woman he was referring to over near the debris, in search of some small reminder to keep as a memento of a part of her life, now gone. How we try to hang on to the beloved past!

The following day, when I reached the crest of the hill on my way to the site, the same county workmen were there and recognized me, after they stopped my car so that a highlift could move some dirt out of the way.

I rolled down my car window and greeted them. One handed me a plowshare he had just dug up and also a portion of the epitaph from an old gravestone that had fallen into the ditch and had become embedded in the dirt. And suddenly I recalled my departed friend, Miss Bessie, who had passed this way once and had wanted to pull out the cherry saplings so that the stones would not crack and crumble into the road the way this one had. I looked over at the little cemetery that had caught her attention that day and wondered how many more markers were hidden beneath the surface, crushed by the heavy foot of time.

Engrossed with these vivid memories, I took a brush and dust pan, and began to clean up the loose dirt from the bottom of my square. (There's no getting away from housework—not even out here, I thought as I swept up the remainder of the soil.)

The helicopter hovered close over us now and started to land.

A crowd began to gather. I noticed some of the officers and members of the Westmoreland County Historical Society. They were talking to State Senator Paul Mahady, who happened to be visiting the site this day. The restoration of Hanna's Town had long been the envisioned dream of them and so many others who had worked hard to get this project off the ground.

Now everyone stood looking up as the chopper came down to land. In its descent it whipped the air about so furiously that it made the grass lie flat on the ground and the ears of the barking dogs were pinned back by the whirlwind it created.

At last the noisy whirleybird settled down upon the field like a tired hen; and in due time several men with camera equipment emerged from the cockpit. They had been photographing the fort site from the air.

Photography—both aerial and close-up—is another important phase of archeology. A photographer in an airplane can record outstanding features of the terrain from this higher elevation. And pertinent information can be gained that cannot be observed from the ground. By viewing the topography of the land from afar, building sites can sometimes be detected. And by using infra-red photography, dark areas on the picture may reveal where a structure was once located. (Occasionally these features can be seen with the naked eye as well. For places of former occupation usually show up as deeper colors in fields when viewed from a distance. Crops will grow differently depending upon what is beneath the surface of the ground. The plant growth will be luxurious over the garbage-enriched soil of the filled-in area, but over walls and foundations that have been covered with subsoil or places scraped bare of topsoil, it tends to be poorer.)

When using close-up photography in archeology, it is essential for everything to be clean and neat so that no feature is obscured. For example, grass and weeds along the edges of a square should be removed before any photographs are taken.

After ground has been exposed to the sun for a period of time, it dries and bleaches white. In order to accentuate such prominences as post-molds and trenches, wetting them with a brush and a bucket of water before they are photographed helps to bring out the features.

Another trick to remember when photographing a section of a square or anything that you want to emphasize, is to include a human figure or an object such as a trowel or a ruler in the picture. This helps convey the actual size of the feature for comparisons.

For recording purposes, a sign or chalk board should be used to identify the site, the square, the date, and the depth of the level in the photograph. And a grid system (nails either secured in the ground or on a frame and placed at six-inch intervals with mason's twine stretched between them) helps when it is superimposed over a feature. A section can be photographed and sketched more accurately this way.

After the helicopter started its motor again and began to rise, once more whipping the grass and barking dogs into a frenzy, we all stood below and watched the great bird until it was but a speck in the sky.

I looked at Pat's watch. Five hours had elapsed from the moment that we had first started that day. I used to think that two hours was long for digging. And yet this is nothing to the time that many of the others give. I could remember years ago wondering how Wayne could spend half a day playing golf and never tire of it. Perhaps on the course the feel of grass underfoot is his own personal contact with nature. Now all of a sudden and at long last I began to understand.

13 • ROLLING STONES

And dance as dust before the sun,
And light of foot, and unconfined,
Hurry from road to road, and run
About the errands of the wind.

And every mote, on earth or air,
Will speed and gleam, down later days.
And like a secret pilgrim fare
By eager and invisible ways.

RUPERT BROOKE

Twenty years is a long time on anyone's calendar. And if memory serves me right, it was about two decades ago that I had written to a journalist, Acker Petit, about a story for the Pittsburgh Press. I was in high school at the time and had read a feature article by Mr. Petit concerning the George Junior Republic—a boy's correctional institute in Grove City, Pennsylvania—my home town. It was a good article, but I knew about another independent organization in the same community—and just as noteworthy. It was a newly refurbished youth center—a run-down old skating rink completely renovated, thanks to the town fathers and a dedicated couple by the name of Vogan. They had a good rapport with the youth. The center, partially operated by the young people, was a big success. Actually it functioned as a deterrent to juvenile delinquency, and I felt that there was a story to be told on behalf of the community's youth center, too. The writer read my letter and decided to cover the story. At the time I was out of town and did not have a chance to meet the author. But I saved the article over the years, although the newspaper is now yellowed with age.

Remembering this, I began to think what a great story there is to tell about Hanna's Town—a small Revolutionary wartime village that disappeared completely like the fantasy of Brigadoon.

Perhaps time had put a cincture on this journalist's mind, and he would not be receptive to others' interests any more. Or maybe he had moved away—or was no longer living, for I had not seen his byline in the Press since I was in my teens.

I wrote to him once again after this lapse of time, sending him a souvenir of the Hanna's Town dig—my lucky stone, on which I had painted a tiny owl. And I told him about the exciting archeological excavations that were taking place at Hanna's Town.

Now, how was I to know that he had used a pseudonym years ago and was no longer writing under a fictitious name? By a stroke of luck I had written to one of Western Pennsylvania's most devoted historians and folklorists. Was it a coincidence, too, that he was a collector of stones? He came out to see the excavations, and in a short period of time two features appeared in the Press. One was a story about the folklore of owls. And, behold, there was my Hanna's Town lucky stone owl staring at me from the page of the newsprint.

The other article began like this:
Broken glass and dishes, rusty iron and tarnished brass, coins, buttons, charcoal and other long-neglected materials are telling a fascinating story today—the story of old Hanna's Town.

As the narration continued, I began to visualize for the first time what actually happened when Hanna's Town was attacked on July 13, 1782.

Up until now, it had merely been historical facts about the burning that I had heard from time to time. And often I, too, had related these same events to visitors at the site—much like a parrot mimicking words from hearsay, without much thought about the emotion or feelings which must have been in the hearts of those people on that fateful day.

I wondered what it must have been like for the young girl, Peggy Shaw, who lived in Hanna's Town when this occurred. What was she doing the afternoon the hundred Seneca

Indians and white tories dressed as savages struck the village? I tried to put myself in her place—a journey into time.

* * *

What a beautiful day for a weddin' at Miller's. And I have to stay at home to help Sarah with the laundry. Wish there was no such thing as having to do the washing and ironing.

For it's Peggy do this and Peggy do that. And lend a hand to Sarah with this and . . . then when I complain, Ma has to add to it: "Lazy bones! Dost thou think God would have given thee arms and legs, if he had not design'd thou should'st use them? Since thou art not sure of a minute, throw not away an hour."

How many times I have used this smoothing-iron on my old linen petticoat! Would that I might have a nice new silk dress for my birthday. One like Jeanette Hanna's.

Seems strangely quiet today, with so many gone to the weddin' party. The only ones I've seen all day are the harvesters with their scythes over in Mr. Huffnagle's field.

Is that Dave's voice I hear outside? The way he's been out scouting the border as a ranger ever since he returned from the army, I hardly have a chance to talk to him anymore. It's not like when we were younger. He always had time to chaff and tease me then.

What's that? Something terrible must have happened, the way everyone is screaming. I wonder if it could be the Indians that Pa's been so worried about lately? . . *Indians!*— in Huffnagle's field! We must run for our lives! There's not even time to gather up anything to take to the fort. Oh, there's my brother now . . .

"Dave, are you sure Pa's safe inside the fort? I didn't see him go in. Oh, thank goodness, there he is. At least the family's all together now."

The noise of the guns . . . the shooting . . . will it ever stop?

Oh—there goes that Moore child, over near the picketing. He'll surely be killed. He's in the direct line of fire . . . Always running off like that, not listening to his mother.

"Jamey! Come here! You'll be killed!" Oh, thank God, I caught him.

"Oh—no!" . . . I can hardly breathe. What's happened! I'm so dizzy. Who's carrying me? Why must everyone crowd 'round me so? . . . I don't want to die!

*   *   *

A bullet from an Indian's rifle had struck Peggy in the right breast and penetrated her lung. The pain must have been insufferable, for they did not have clean clinical conditions and could use only unskilled backwoods surgery. A silk handerchief was drawn back and forth through the wound to remove the discharge.

Who would guess what her thoughts were if she had been conscious during the nightmarish attack? Had she heard that a group of Indians, upon discovering that they could not harm the settlers in the fort, had left the others and set off for Miller's blockhouse to kill and capture the inhabitants there? I wonder if she was cognizant of the Indians burning to the ground all but the fort and two of the houses in Hanna's Town?

Could she hear the yelling and all the commotion as the raiders looted their homes—with almost light touches at times, such as when an Indian tried to put on the Hanna girl's silk dress by sticking his foot through the sleeve; or when one proudly strutted around in a bright military jacket he had discovered in one of the cabins, until he was shot down by someone from inside the fort?

Did she hear the drums that beat that night within the stockade walls while men from the neighboring settlement rode back and forth across a bridge to deceive the savages into thinking there were many reinforcements coming in under cover of darkness?

Was she conscious the next morning when the plan worked and the enemy had at last gone, leaving the town in smouldering ashes and strewn with carcasses of animals either burned or shot during the battle?

The only thing that we do know for sure is that Peggy wasted away and died about two weeks later. Today a stone marks her grave at the old Middle Presbyterian Church yard, in the nearby community of Mt. Pleasant.

Suddenly I recalled the young girl I had seen at Hanna's Town that spring morning a few years ago. How she had vanished just as quickly and mysteriously as she had appeared that day. How my mind had easily succumbed to fantasy surrounded by history and ghosts of the past.

My thoughts returned to the conclusion of the article:

Almost prophetic were the words written three decades ago by Agnes Sligh Turnbull in 'The Day Must Dawn,' a novel about Hanna's Town and its people.

In the book, a pioneer woman writes in her diary:

"I keep wondering in the watches of the night if them that come after will know and care, and think on all that we have gone through. It would make it easier if we knew they would. But who can tell?"

Rest well in your earthy bed, O brave pioneers. Someone does know and care, even after two centuries have passed.

No longer using a pen name, Dr. George Swetnam—the real author of the article—could not have written any truer words.

With the passing of years we did not forget the pioneers. There was too much to forget. As James Matthews wrote long ago:

Above their dust the wind howls dolefully,
  And the last coon-skin moulders on the wall;
  All, all are gone,—and darkness, like a pall,
Steals o'er the mem'ry of the pioneers;
We reap the fruitage of their bitter years.
And o'er their slumbers deep, outpour the
  meed of tears.

Too much to forget and so very much to do. All the original buildings have vanished over the years, but newly constructed ones have risen from the ashes like a phoenix on the wing. Today as one drives down over Gallows Hill on the old Forbes Road, the first thing that comes in view is a rustic frontier fort—a stockade made of logs hand-hewn and debarked with draw knives, and inside the beginning of a so-called blockhouse, all built by volunteers. We all got into the act—men, women, and children. I can still see Pat and me scraping bark off of some of those logs. Many hours of human labor went into the new fort as it had been with the fort of years gone by.

Across from the stockade a small round-log jail, built to the recorded description of the original, now serves as a gift shop at the site—once a place of agony, now a pleasant looking edifice.

And next to the jail is the new Robert Hanna courthouse-tavern, reminiscent of the late 1700s. The framework was built symbolically in one day's time by teams of firemen and other volunteers from all over the county (in the same manner that it was accomplished years ago at a log cabin raising, during the county's bicentennial.) Each log was hand-hewn from oak trees, and every shingle made on an old-fashioned schnitzelbank, previous to the time of its erection and all under the expert direction of contractor and friend of the historical society, Carl Schultz, affectionately known as "Huck." And given time there will be others built. After almost two centuries Old Hanna's Town is coming to life again.

Not long ago Wayne and I drove by the restoration on the evening of an early winter snow. I recalled that it was not quite Christmas when we had had our first winter storm the year they built the tavern. It was on such a night as this that we were on a lonely country road on our way to the reconstructed inn for a pioneer dinner, prepared by the women of the Elizabeth Hanna Guild of the Westmoreland County Historical Society. (These industrious hard-working women also present style shows for the public, using authentically designed clothing in keeping with the Hanna's Town period, and they hold antique marts throughout the summer months at the fort site.)

I shall long remember the view of that log house as we descended the hill. It stood in the darkness, warm and inviting against a snowy background. Every window glowed with candlelight, and smoke curled from its massive stone chimney. It was like a peaceful refuge in a storm. And I could imagine the relief that travelers must have felt in bygone days upon reaching their destination after hours of exposure to the cold winds. For us, we had the comfort of a warm automobile; but they would have come by horseback or in drafty wagons, if not afoot.

I had lingered a while before entering and joining the festivities that evening. How this lonely spot had swarmed with thousands of people, watching the structure being built that summer for the bicentennial of the county's founding. Now the hurly-burly of the crowds was gone, and their voices mingled and were lost with those from the earlier past. Only the wind echoed through the frozen trees.

I remembered the large, mysterious stone that I had uncovered in my first days of digging. Now, on this very same location stood another building—the Hanna's Town courthouse-tavern. Two hundred years later it stands as a replica of the first seat of law and order west of the Allegheny Mountains. And it was right where I had discovered what seemed to be a boulder in the beginning days of the dig. Perhaps one of the original logs from the courthouse had once rested on its surface.

Now furnished with eighteenth-century antiques, a new old-fashioned hostelry rekindles memories of the days when people knew nothing about gasoline, let alone a shortage of it; back in the times when grease lamps were burned, because tallow was scarce. This log structure stands as a constant witness that the early settlers' lives were simple and meager, compared to ours. Seeing it we are reminded that they, too, had hardships and shortages. Luxuries we know today were unheard of back then. And although our lifestyles have already changed and will change even more because of nature's depletion and humankind's wastefulness, it is like an ever-present symbol to us that we too can—and shall—endure.

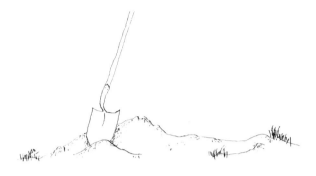

14 • EARTHWORKS

O world, I cannot hold thee close enough!
Thy winds, thy wide gray skies!
Thy mists that roll and rise!
Thy woods, this autumn day, that ache and sag
And all but cry with color!...
. . . .
World, world, I cannot get thee close enough!
EDNA ST. VINCENT MILLAY

Assiduously volunteers continue to search for more artifacts and look for any lead that may reveal information about the early settlers of Hanna's Town. And it is interesting to follow the development of those around me. Others, like myself, had sought more enrichment in life. They, too, have found it in working through history, and have grown and reached out as a result of it. In so doing we have discovered that living creatively with a goal, one never does "come of age"—and as someone has said, "But, oh the journey!"

In retrospect, I wasn't alone out there, as I had wondered about years ago when first commencing this project. Others had searched and found fulfillment, too, in what had started out to be a "dig" and ended up as a monumental task of rebuilding a village and solving the mystery of its former inhabitants.

By now some of the volunteers and members of the Westmoreland County Historical Society had written a number of pamphlets, research inventories, and books—all related to or a result of their interest in Hanna's Town—Ed,

Ann, Jean, Kathy, and Millie. Others were busy working as tour guides and wore costumes they had made from authentic patterns of the eighteenth century—Drew, Ethel, Jean, Lee, Mildred, and Nancy, to name a few. Pete, Ray, Don, Jack, Bob and Wib, among others, had their own pioneer clothing too.

And of course there was young Pete from Hannastown. Something great happened in Pete's life. One day he called to me from his bike as he approached the site where I was working at Hanna's Town. "Guess what, Helene!" Pete's enthusiasm bubbled over once more as he told me all about the community college he was going to attend and what subjects he would be taking. And in due time it was, "Guess what" again, and he was telling me about his new job. But the big news came one day when he announced "Guess what, Helene!" and before I could respond he said, "I'm getting married!" Pete had not only found an interest in archeology, but he had also found himself a wife, Annette, a fellow volunteer at Hanna's Town. And as it turned out they were married in the log courthouse-tavern in an old-fashioned wedding with period attire. Second to be married on the historic site was Mildred's daughter, followed by others inspired by Hanna's Town.

It is interesting, in retrospect, how working at a historic site could change one's life. Not only did I become enthralled with Hanna's Town along with others like me, but I also began to branch out and research landmarks elsewhere— starting in Westmoreland County and reaching to other sections of the state as well, which resulted in the production and publication of a number of historical dramas and books, two of which were written about Hanna's Town. And it all started out by answering an ad about digging in the dirt! I have become so hooked on history and just plain getting back to earth that we now live on a farm in a nineteenth century house located near Hanna's Town—making plans to reconstruct an authentic historic log cabin on our property. In addition to Brigette we are now raising an angora goat, a lamb, geese, ducks, and a few chickens, although Wayne says (in jest) the only thing that he wants to raise is his golf club. (Actually he raises a fine garden, in between rounds of golf.)

Besides interesting sites and beautiful people, I have discovered in my travels fascinating, hidden places off the well-beaten paths which I otherwise would not have found. And the nice thing about this is that anyone can do the same thing wherever he or she lives. We are living in the midst of a rich heritage—for our very own country is chock-full of history and excitement. As the song says, happiness lies, "right in your own backyard."

So very many of these charming, wayside places are nearby. I had at one time wanted to go to a distant land in search of adventure, while all the time it was right here—waiting to be discovered. Again I thought of something James Matthews had written:

> There's a world of grander themes
> Than the dead ol' days and dreams
>   Trampled in the dust of Greece
>   Or of Rome—
>   You can find it, if you please,
>   Nearer home.

For years I had thought that adventure was somewhere beyond my reach, while all the time the pastures were green on my side of the fence, too.

For some reason we seldom make an effort to see the interesting places in our own community. We have become accustomed to traveling great distances to satisfy our adventuresome appetites. But to an outsider, our very surroundings are a source of endless fascination. We are blinded by familiarity. Perhaps with the realization that the world's natural resources are rapidly being used up by the masses of population (bringing about shortages of gasoline, gas, and oil) we will begin to appreciate our own neighborhoods, since it has become essential for us to limit our travel. And we will take the blinders off our eyes and begin to see the interesting world close to home.

Back in the 1700s when the early naturalists were busy exchanging seeds between the colonies and England, a nuisance plant called plain-weed was sent to the mother country. The people there were so impressed by its beauty that they planted it in exclusive locations in the great gardens of the royal palace for everyone to see and admire.

And in 1816 William Cobbett wrote in *The American Gardener*: " . . . Hampton Court, where, growing in a rich soil to the height of five or six feet, it, under the name of 'Golden Rod,' nods over the whole length of the edge of the walk, three quarters of a mile long, and perhaps, thirty feet wide, the most magnificent . . . in Europe."

Sir William Osler stated it best when he said: "Nothing will sustain you more potently than the power to recognize in your humdrum routine—as perhaps it may be thought the true poetry of life—the poetry of the commonplace, of the ordinary man . . ."

While I was working at Hanna's Town one day, a demon-like dragon fly decided to land beside me in my square. Although it looked grotesque, there was a certain beauty in it. The head was green and the tail blue, quite a marvel in itself, since for many years these two colors were usually considered discordant. Whoever started that theory must surely have been daffy. God, in all His glory, created that mini-monster and placed it against a backdrop of blue sky and green grass. And nature is never inharmonious or color-blind. Perhaps Oswald Spengler expressed the color concept best when he wrote, "Blue and green are the colors of the heavens, the sea, the fruitful plain, the shadow of the southern noon, the evening, the remote mountains."

This background has since become my canvas of life, with the azure sky as my ceiling, the warm green timber my walls, and beneath my feet a carpet of grass. Not only out-of-doors, but indoors as well I had subconsciously chosen that color scheme many years before. Although the tempo and tone have changed somewhat, I have become on intimate terms with nature, once more learning to live life at its fullest, as I did in my youth.

And in digging up the shattered ceramics at Hanna's Town, I have even begun to look at humanity with a new perspective—placing together broken pieces of earth to solve the puzzle of human history. Just like the shards of pottery that we try to repair, so people can be compared to broken pieces of china, striving to be whole and complete. We are all made from the same dust on this earth and derived from the same clay—though fired and tempered differently. Whether we are light, dark, coarse or fine, God has given life to us to do with as we see fit. The digging and researching have taught me this full respect for the essence of humankind and the mosaic of creative life.

I have discovered that redware is no less beautiful than creamware or pearlware. Earthenware, though coarse, is rugged and durable. Yet all are made for utility. Though greatly diversified, we are all bound together as human beings, living in the same period of time. Our yesterdays will always follow us, and we cannot really know ourselves and others without first knowing our past. To state that history is meaningless is like saying memory has no value. For that is what history is all about—the memory of yesterdays and many more to come.

History is the key to our past and the control of our future. The knowledge uncovered through archeology gives a fuller meaning to life—a means of understanding who and what we are.

I have learned to love the earth and its people. And getting down to earth—bound as I am with my eyes on the stars and my feet on the ground—here is where I shall stay to continue with my digging, research, and recording of history, until I, too, am enclosed within the bounds of clay which may then reveal the world's entire mystery.

Besides, what else is there for a golf widow to do?

DIGGING UP HANNA'S TOWN—The author and Brigette.
Photo by James Klingensmith, Pittsburgh Post-Gazette

DIGGING UP THE PAST—Jake Grimm and Pete Cholock.

Photo by John Gibson, Valley News Dispatch

ANTICIPATION—Guide and young visitors at the fort site just before the fort was rebuilt.

Photo by John Gibson, Valley News Dispatch

STEPPING INTO HISTORY—Guides and visitors at the Hanna's Town courthouse.

Photo by John Gibson, Valley News Dispatch

THE EVOLUTION OF PROHIBITION
IN THE UNITED STATES OF AMERICA